RELATIONAL AGGRESSION

AND ITS NEGATIVE EFFECTS

ON YOUNG GIRLS

By Yvette Michelle Apodaca, M.A.

Ordering Information:
To order additional copies of this book, please visit:
https://www.createspace.com/4540001

Table of Contents

DEDICATION

To my three daughters:
Ashley, Miranda, and Analisa.

Ashley, you have been my inspiration to write this book. I thank you for sharing your stories with me, and I know it was difficult. I watch you, now, as you fulfill your role as a mother, wife and friend. You have grown to be a beautiful, loving and giving person. You have beaten the odds and overcame the horrible effects of relational aggression, and I commend you. You have been a wonderful daughter, as you have supported me and helped me with your younger sisters when I needed you. Thank you for always being there.

Miranda, you have also been my inspiration for writing this book. Thank you for sharing your story with me. You amaze me with everything you have accomplished. Thank you for all your support throughout my Pacific Oaks journey. You have been understanding and have become very independent to make sure that I could continue my education.

My little Analisa, you too have been my inspiration. Your story touched me and gave me the power to continue writing this book. You were so helpful throughout this writing process, as you always shared your concerns for people at school that were being bullied. You showed so much interest in what I was writing that I knew in my heart, I chose a perfect topic to write about. Thank you, Analisa, for encouraging me with your love and support.

To all the girls that participated in the interview process. Your stories touched my life in so many ways. When this book was completed, I sat in a quiet place and reflected on all your pain and voices that were so strong and eager to be heard. Because of you, this book was a success. Because of you, many girls will be saved. Thank you for sharing such a difficult part of your young life. You each have a place in my heart.

FORWARD

My whole purpose for writing this book is to explore relational aggression and its effects on school-age and adolescent girls. Through the use of in depth study and research, illumination of the hidden dynamics of female bullying will take place. This book will also provide knowledge of the available resources for parents and educators.

Included in this book is a resource guide for parents and teachers, which discusses the signs of a child that has been bullied, as well as pertinent information to assist families and classrooms in relational aggression prevention and intervention.

The topic of relational aggression amongst adolescent females is significant, as it is destroying the psychological wellbeing of girls on an international scale. Mistreatment and subsequent bullying are commonplace in the school system, and this book offers parents and educators a support system as they begin to better understand the severity of relational aggression and its irreversible, long-term effects on adolescent development.

Prevention and intervention are imperative, as highlighted in this book. As one begins to understand the effects of the bully's actions and the adult reactions, a profile of the aggressor and bystander is highlighted for a comprehensive view of relational aggression in the school context.

1

A PERSONAL PROBLEM

*"Mommy, my heart hurts because my friends don't want
to play with me, anymore. I have no more friends!"* ~Jada age:5

The human experience can be traumatic, and due to this, most people hide from difficult emotions, rather than face them. We run from the destruction that can come with the pain. We dodge and avoid it by trying to feel nothing, at all.

Is that the right approach? Is it wrong? As we watch our youth drowning in despair and pain, I think the better question would be how do we stop this? How do we help?

On November 10th, 2000, I was shocked by what I viewed on the news broadcast. A fourteen year-old girl, Dawn Marie Wesley, took her own life shortly after three adolescent girls called her on the telephone. Apparently, Dawn had been experiencing psychological and verbal abuse from the schoolmates on a daily basis. What was so heartbreaking was the fact that these girls were in her *closest* circle of friends.

My first thought was, how could this abuse have gone so far? How could this type of abuse happen and no one realize that she was in trouble? I wondered about the people she was in contact with on a daily basis: her parents, teachers, friends, and neighbors. How was it possible for them to apparently be so blind to her plight? I just could not understand.

After researching this story further, I discovered that her mother was also unaware of the verbal and emotional abuse that her daughter endured until it was too late. Dawn never confided in her mother, or anyone else for that matter. Despite some at school being aware of the abuse, no one acted or attempted to protect Dawn.

As I delved further into researching bullying, peer intimidation, and harassment, it became clear that this is not an uncommon situation. There were literally thousands of incidents of bullying, especially at the adolescent stage of development.

Fearing retaliation and further humiliation, those that are bullied choose to suffer in silence, rather than expose their situation. This silence worsens their predicament. Many parents are left in the dark, unaware of the relational aggression and how it impacts their child.

This problem touched my family, as well, but with different results than the Wesley case. I, too, was unaware of my daughter's situation at school, and while I prided myself on the close relationship I had maintained with my daughter throughout her school age years, I was horrified to discover that she never shared her suffering with me. My story parallels that of countless other parents that discover that their child has been the victim of relational aggression.

My eleven-year-old daughter, Miranda, would oftentimes come to me complaining of stomach pains, headaches, and rashes on various parts of her body. I assumed there must be an infection or a virus going around. At some point in time, we visited her physician three times in one month for these generalized pains! The doctor could not find anything physically wrong with Miranda, so we were sent on our way with recommendations to get more rest.

Continuing to complain of stomach aches and headaches, my daughter began to miss more and more days of school. Out of frustration and concern, I scheduled another appointment with the physician. Curled up in a fetal position, Miranda lay on the examination table, waiting to be seen. Hoping that we would receive a concrete diagnosis, this time, I anxiously waited with my daughter.

When the doctor came in, she began asking Miranda questions. She inquired about Miranda's social life at school, and when she asked her if she had friends at school, Miranda answered, "No" in a low tone.

Proceeding with more questions, the doctor inquired about her closer relationships with her peers. Embarrassed, Miranda admitted that she did not have one best friend. Shocked at what I was hearing, I felt my stomach tighten with a sick feeling. Miranda's diagnosis and treatment did not consist of the usual over the counter medication, rest, and reassurance that "she will be fine with time". No, Miranda was suffering from an incurable epidemic. This epidemic infects children, regardless of age, ethnicity, and ability. This epidemic is relational aggression, or bullying.

The day after our visit to the doctor and diagnosis of stress induced by bullying, I dropped Miranda off at school. I watched as she walked past the entrance gate and into the schoolyard. A group of girls the same age as Miranda were huddled together, whispering and laughing loudly as Miranda walked towards them. As she went to speak to them, the girls scattered in different directions. The look on Miranda's face spoke louder than words, and I died inside as I watched it unfold before my eyes. She slouched and walked with her head down as she slowly went to class. My daughter, usually cheerful and poised, had become a child that I would have never recognized.

At this time, everything began to make sense to me. Miranda was usually outgoing, happy, and friendly, but lately, she had been exhibiting signs of withdrawal and isolation, at home. She had become a child that was oftentimes complaining, moody, and was relentlessly picking on her younger sister.

Miranda's grades in school were also beginning to show signs of distress. I had reasoned that Miranda was going through adolescent angst, believing that these were signs of normal adolescent behavior. If I had only known that my daughter was suffering so much at school. The guilt that I experienced was overwhelming! Blaming myself, I felt that I should have been more aware of my daughter's circumstances. It is something that I continue to struggle with. However, writing about adolescent relational aggression is healing.

Similar to my daughter, many girls fall victim to relational aggression, or bullying. These distrustful female relationships have a powerful influence on how girls interpret and perccive female friendships. Because of this, my daughter was stripped of the innocence and joy of close female friendships. Having special friends to share your most intimate thoughts, fantasies, and slumber parties lends itself to positive growth and development. However, my daughter and countless other girls like her, encounter low self esteem, distrust, and isolation in place of friendship. The effects are long-term, affecting all aspects of emotional and social development.

The passage of time has not healed the wounds of relational aggression for my daughter, Miranda. As she began high school, Miranda chose to socialize primarily with males, instead of females, lamenting that the females in the school are "mean". When I asked her who she likes to spend a lot of time with at school, she answered, "A lot of people". Although I was not totally convinced of her happiness with these relationships, I was somewhat relieved to hear that she at least had some friends. I was, however, still concerned that she lacked faith in her female counterparts. Of course, Miranda is not alone in her feelings. Female relational aggression is on the rise and continues to damage the full scope of adolescence.

2

No, It's Not Normal

"I couldn't concentrate. I was always scared, and I kept hearing her voice in my head, yelling at me and calling me names." ~Marlena, age:14

Have you ever heard someone say, "Boys will be boys" or "Girls will be girls"? It isn't uncommon for people to take the stance that female bullying is just something that "all girls do." The reaction and a lack of reaction to female aggression by well-intentioned parents and educators lead to tragic results. The old adage that "sticks and stones may break my bones, but names will never hurt me" is a fallacy. In fact, the death of Dawn Wesley and other adolescents who have been bullied speaks to the danger of "names".

While it is true that "sticks and stones" do lead themselves to physical pain, verbal and emotional abuse are as serious as physical abuse, if not more because of its insidious nature. Bullying need not necessarily be physical, which is far easier to identify. Relational aggression, in its verbal and emotional context, is extremely harmful to female psychological well-being.

Some of the emotional signs of relational aggression are being withdrawn, insecurity, low self-esteem, shame, fear, anxiety, and impaired academic performance. Suicidal ideation and attempts are the more serious consequences of relational aggression. These and other conditions have dramatic effects on the female adolescents' development throughout the lifespan.

In order to have strong and healthy mothers, wives, friends, daughters, and professionals, it is critical that action be taken to reverse this horrible trend. Relational aggression is counterproductive and destructive to development. Lacking trust, safety, and self-esteem, the woman bullied as a youth is psychologically unhealthy and less likely to forge and maintain healthy relationships with others.

Until the 1900s, it was assumed that girls were "nicer" than boys and that they did not engage in relational aggression to the extent that boys do. Nothing could be further from the truth, though. Researchers have discovered that female aggression is potentially more harmful than the physical aggression that males tend to engage in. The male schoolyard bully will harass and torment a particular child through verbal and physical aggression, which is damaging. However, female bullies cunningly attack the most vulnerable part of a female's development: their socialization.

Over the years, we have seen an increase in female aggression, bullying and general violence. Newspapers, magazines, radio, television, and motion pictures have highlighted this mean girl syndrome that is become more and more blatant. Even though this is the case, it isn't being taken as seriously as it should.

Culturally, there is a denial of the seriousness of female aggression, which has caused it to become an epidemic. Because of there being a refusal to allow girls access to open conflict, it turns into a sneaky battle of venom and spite. Backbiting, backstabbing, rumors, name calling, manipulation, and open exclusion are used in order to inflict psychological pain on the victim. Relationships, even ones that are supposed to be close, are not sacred, anymore.

Girls will sit in the safety of their own group of friends to poke fun at their victim. It doesn't stop there, though, because the friends who surround the instigator join in on the "fun". What starts out as one girl attacking another turns into a pack of verbal wolves attacking one girl. This, of course, intensifies the damage that is inflicted.

The most common forms of bullying involve taunts, name-calling, gossip, and threats. In my own experience, as well as the experience of others, adults do not take these forms of bullying very seriously, at all. The scars from this type of bullying might not be as visible as the scars of physical violence, but they are there and have a powerful effect on the psyche. For most girls, social ostracisms are far more hurtful than a physical blow to the face.

There are so many myths about bullying, as well, which causes problems with attempting to eradicate this issue. Parents and teachers sometimes succumb to these myths and end up telling children that are suffering from bullying:

"Just ignore it."

"Bullying happens all the time."

"They'll move on to someone else."

It blinds parents and teachers to what is truly happening to the child, inside, and the child experiences mistrust as a result of the lack of communication and lack of adult action on the child's behalf. Because of this, children tend to internalize the suffering because the adult has not taken the bullying seriously. They fear being labeled as a tattletale or a snitch, and the child keeps their suffering to themselves. After all, no one likes a tattletale.

Over the years, there have been many surveys conducted about bullying, and in many of them, half of the children that were bullied have admitted to telling no one. Of the children that did share their plight with a trusted adult, almost half of them admitted to telling a parent, while many of the others told a teacher. The results from these studies speak to the fact that in a child's mind, telling on a bully implies weakness and failure. Essentially, it speaks of fear.

They're fearful that the bully may discover that they have exposed her. Perhaps, the child reasons that the bully will retaliate with even more fury. Who will be there to provide protection at that time? If you have dealt with bullying, yourself, you may know that fear of retaliation is the most effective form of bribery and secrecy.

What if you end up getting a combination like this:

1) A bully who gets what she wants from her target, a target who is afraid to tell...

2) Bystanders who watch, participate, or look away...

3) And adults who interpret the bullying as harmless "teasing", who assume that bullying is a normal part of growing up…

Wouldn't this be a deadly combination?

In addition to the helplessness and hopelessness felt by the bullied child, the parent is also left unaware of their child's plight. When the children and adults in the child's life are apathetic to their suffering, the child feels vulnerable and alone.

In recent years, we have had schools step up with mottos that state that children have the right to attend a school that is safe, has a rewarding environment, and is free of ridicule and shame; in other words, a no-tolerance to bullying.

Is this what is happening, though?

3

IS IT REALLY THAT BAD?

*"I feel bad about myself all the time, and I am ashamed
that I can't speak up. Sometimes, I feel like I don't
belong in school." Marlena, age:14*

Generally speaking, research has proven that all aspects of bullying are harmful to the health and well-being of children. Although viewed by many as a childhood rite of passage, it is far from the "rite of passage" that many adults associate with the teenage years. Instead, it is a form of abuse which leaves behind scars. Particularly, female bullying has received attention as a widespread problem. One must only glance at headline after headline over the last ten years to see this problem being brought to light.

Popularity, physical appearance, and acceptance encompass female relational aggression as the offender seeks to destroy the social life of her intended victim. Because of this, female bullying is oftentimes explained as the use of relationships in order to inflict pain.

While physical aggression has more visible cues, relational aggression presents a challenge due to its more subtle nature. Some characteristics of this type of bullying can be seen in rumors, gossip, backbiting, being socially excluded, and the formation of tight-knit cliques that target other girls.

Because social development is so important, the prevention of female alliances is devastating and has deep consequences. Isolation occurs for these young girls, and this deprives them of their most important support systems, their peers.

There have been countless studies done over the years, and these investigations are unanimous in many of their findings:

- Relationally aggressive behavior is evident in all age groups, from preschool to adulthood.
- Females are more apt to display relational aggression in their social circles than males, who aggress outside of their friendship circle.
- Relationally aggressive girls are less likely to show empathy for others.
- Girls are more likely to approve of and use relational aggression, while boys are more likely to approve of and use physical aggression.
- Relational aggression is connected to peer rejection, decreased acts of pro-social behavior, and anti-social and borderline personality features in young adults.

In studies conducted with children from **grades three through eight**, it has been found that as high as one in three children are victims of relational aggression. This is a staggering amount, and in interviews done with these children, it has been found that they exhibited many similar problems:

- Not feeling safe at school.
- Not wanting to go to school because of bullying.
- Not feeling that adults really cared about them.

It has also been concluded that girls experience relational aggression more often than boys, and older students are more likely to use relational aggression to their vantage point than younger children.

In studies conducted with children from **grades eight through twelve**, studies have concluded some interesting finds about that age group when it comes to bullying:

- Being left out of activities with their peers.
- Being called hurtful names.
- Teasing.
- Experience of physical violence.
- Verbal and non-verbal threats.
- Cyber-bullying (through internet and cellular phone messages).

The years have given us so much knowledge about this important social issue for children, and while both boys and girls are affected, it is a tragic occurrence when these things are leading to the death of so many of our youth.

If you have ever experienced any of these issues that have been discussed, then I am sure you understand the pain and hurt involved. In the next Chapter, we will discuss childhood development, which will give us a glimpse into the critical stages that children go through.

4

PEERS ARE IMPORTANT

"I feel like I'm not wanted and I don't belong in school. I feel depressed every day and I don't care about anything, not myself, school, just nothing!" ~Jessy, age:12

C hildhood blossoms into the teen years, and this is an important time for children to learn important social skills that will serve them in the coming years that will lead them into adulthood. Whether it be with jobs, marriages, adult friendships, or raising children of their own, these skills are essential for success and self-confidence. The quality of life is most definitely affected by bullying.

It is important to be able to connect with others in close friendships that have an exchange of healthy intimate knowledge. When children have strong friendships like these, healthy relational habits are formed which extend beyond such close friendships, allowing them to interact in a healthy manner with others around them. These positive peer relations enhance psychosocial development and last a lifetime. It is a time where skills are mastered, goals are accomplished, and children become more industrious.

Because of this crucial area of development, it represents an area of crisis as the child struggles with unresolved feelings of inadequacy and inferiority in peer relationships. This creates a potential for weak links in self esteem.

Children that are school age begin to mature, emotionally. If they feel sadness, they are more able to alleviate the sadness by thinking more positive thoughts or finding something that interests them, like a hobby. They begin to have the confidence to develop friendships and extend consideration, empathy, and compassion for others. None of this is full-proof, though, since they are still developing these skills. Sometimes, they may act inappropriately, which has the potential to jeopardize these vital friendships.

This lends itself to a greater complexity in the understanding of close relationships and the depth of relationship building, which is a skill that many do not master until adolescence. Their identity, role, relationship building and social acceptance become a juggling issue. Figuring out that their intrapersonal identity (close relationships) in the context of the family and society is challenging. Without supportive intrapersonal relationships, the child in this stage of development will experience role confusion and frustration.

The development of positive relationships allows for clarity in their philosophy of life and goal setting. One way to help this along is for children to join supporting causes through school and community clubs. These clubs, events, and social gatherings help them to develop and maintain intimate peer relationships through a common purpose. This supports one of the most significant relationships, which is the peer connection.

Peer relationships and environmental influence is much like an egg, with the environment as a major influence on relationship building. In the middle, like a yoke, a child will have those relationships that are closest to them. This would include immediate relationships, such as family and school relationships. The interaction between the child and this yoke-like group of people has a profound influence on the child's ability to attain and maintain intimate relationships. The more nurturing this is, the better the growth and development of the child will be.

Many experts stress that the most influential system in which school age and adolescent children develop his or her self esteem is through peer groups, which is a group of individuals who play, work and learn together. Acceptance in one's peer group can potentially enhance the child's sense of competency, particularly in the stage of middle childhood. It is at this time that there is a greater frequency and duration of peer interaction in comparison to other stages of development.

Not surprisingly, children become increasingly dependent on their peers, not only for companionship but also for self validation and advice. These relationships provide unique opportunities for growth in the area of close relationships, as well as within acquaintance relationships. They allow for opportunities to discover proper socialization in behavior, personality, and the ability to adapt in challenging circumstances.

Socialization is a complex path that is essential for development, and by understanding the steps in this process, it can help adults design interventions for children who have been rejected by their peers.

Many studies have shown that children in the **Preschool** years begin to delight in cooperative and shared play. As they age, they become **School** age, where they benefit from larger and more structured positive peer group interactions. Their friendship skills develop as they learn to negotiate issues involving competition, conformity, and achievement. Peer relations are sustained for longer periods, and more stable friendships are created.

As children reach **Preadolescence**, they often experience a need for a special friendship that offers greater emotional intimacy and support. Many form close relationships with same sex peers that provide models for the rewards and demands involved in sustaining close emotional relationships.

Upon reaching **Adolescence**, youth begin to recognize different social styles and norms, which are reflected in "cliques" and "crowds." As youth move in and out of these groups, they have opportunities to explore different facets of the self and are challenged to define their personal values and sense of self. Youth may try on different social roles and experience a range of relationships, helping them to define the kinds of persons they are and the kinds of persons they want to be. Peers also provide emotional support in this confusing time of life, serving as "stepping stones" as adolescents move away from emotional dependence upon their parents and toward the independent functioning that will label them as adults.

I think we can all agree that these stages are critical, and later in this book, I will discuss coping strategies and important resources to aid parents and teachers in the powerful role that they play.

5

FRIENDSHIP AND GIRLS

"One day, she just stopped being my friend and started
hanging around with these girls and just didn't
talk to me, anymore." ~Nicole, age:11

Friendship is that nonsexual connection that happens with others, and it offers social support, a confidant to share emotions and information with, and an opportunity to give that same type of support to others. It chases away the loneliness that occurs due to isolation, and it gives a sense of comfort in social situations.

Many researchers agree that children of all ages tend to choose friends of the same sex. As children become more particular about their friends, their friendship groups begin to shrink.

While most four year olds may say that they have many friends, by the time they hit eight, they will have a small circle of friends. By age ten, most children have one best friend to whom their loyalty is given.

Although this trend toward an increasingly exclusive friendship network is followed by both sexes, it tends to be more evident among females. By the end of middle childhood, many girls have one best friend on whom they depend for social and emotional support.

Girls are socialized to place high value on their relationships with others, and as they enter early adolescence, they learn that developing friendships with other girls is a primary task in their development. Having a strong friendship group is a protective factor for all girls, but especially those at risk of engaging in risky behavior due to environmental factors.

In addition, girls are more likely than boys to value their relationships in several ways. Girls expect and receive more kindness, loyalty, commitment and empathy from friends than do boys. Furthermore, girls report spending more time thinking about friends, having more jealousy and exclusivity in friendships, and experience more negative emotions based on exclusion by their friends, more so than boys. This factor of female peer relationships is highlighted in many works of literature.

Many girls, even as young as seven and eight years old, speak passionately about their feelings of friendship. Strong feelings of loyalty and love for friends are matched only by the anger and pain of fighting and disagreeing with them. It has been reported that experiencing face to face conflict with peers leaves girls feeling saddened in more instances than any other experience they have.

When adults treat girls badly, they have very little option other than to cry "unfair," but when their friends do so, they react by expressing strong feelings, asking questions, or actively protesting. And yet, though these reactions tell of hurt feelings or exclusion, anger, and frustration, they also tell us they are less likely to react to physical violence and more likely to react with verbal outbursts. To girls, words seem to be more powerful to them than physical assault from their peers and close relationships.

All children speak of the trust they feel toward their closest friends and the things they could talk about that they could not discuss with others. Sociologists have speculated that girls' friendships display this intimacy, but boys' relationships are more superficial because they form sites for roughhousing and play, rather than the close bonds that seem to form in female friendships.

Many studies agree that best friends seem especially important to girls during middle school age years because they are like a constant and never-changing stability, while everything else is changing and different. Interestingly, even if a girl has many friends, the lack of a single close friend with whom she can share her deepest secrets can leave her feeling dissatisfied, empty, and lost.

Research on adolescent friendships has shown that positive experiences of friendship and peer relations considerably affect cognitive, social, and moral development. They build the groundwork for attention-building, strengthening memory, producing and understanding language, general learning, reasoning, problem solving, and decision making Positive friendships help girls to adjust well and have good social and emotional health.

Studies have indicated that friendships satisfy the adolescent's desire for emotional intimacy and greatly enhance their interpersonal skills, empathy, and consideration for others. Adolescents who have difficulties finding and maintaining friendships are more likely to be unemployed, aggressive, or have poor mental health as adults. Indeed, close friendships are considered by many social scientists to be the most rewarding and satisfying of all human relations and are clearly important for the social and emotional health of adolescents.

It must be concluded, then, that intimacy (the ability to share one's thoughts and feelings with a friend) is the central feature of adolescent girls' friendships, because girls in early adolescence prefer intensely personal relationships and rely more heavily on their best friend than do boys. Furthermore, girls' friendships become more intimate, self disclosing, and stable over time. The gender differences in quality and stability become more apparent as adolescents grow older.

We see the consequences if this growth is interrupted or halted. Through the countless pieces of news coverage and the countless studies conducted, it creates a void inside of girls, making them yearn for someone to understand them. For many, it leads them into bad situations and pushes them into decisions that they would never had made if they'd had someone to be there for them.

6

REJECTION AND SELF ESTEEM

*"I never wanted to go anywhere. I was afraid that I would
see her, somewhere." ~Marlena, age:14*

Many researchers agree that one of the most common signs of relational aggression is peer rejection. Bullying in this manner alienates and rejects peers and purposefully ruins friendships in subtle manners, like aggressive stares, rolling eyes, heavy sighing, frowns, sneers, snickers, snide remarks, and hostile body language.

The worst time for this type of aggression is in middle school years, where with the onset of adolescence, pre-teens go through many physical, emotional, and sexual changes. During this time, young girls are trying to figure out who they are and trying to fit in with their peers.

This opens up many opportunities for ugly behavior, since puberty causes many transitions with the body. During this time, some teens end up needing glasses, or get severe cases of acne, have weight gain, or grow so much that their limbs cause them to be clumsier than they were, previously.

Names are an attack on a person's character and who they are, and in this stage of life where teens are attempting to find out who they are and who they want to be, it sinks deeply into them. Names like "pizza face," "four-eyes," "fatty," "chicken legs," and worse become common terms that are used to inflict pain. This behavior causes worse problems when the victim involved is a loner. There's no one to turn to or talk to. There's no one to stand up to the aggressors or stand beside them for moral support.

Many things that also happen, socially, include intentionally excluding a child from sleepovers, birthday parties, and playground games. This is often overlooked as a form of bullying because it is not as obvious as name calling or a fist in the face. The results of a black eye or a torn jacket aren't evident, and the pain it causes is usually hidden. When the pain is expressed, though, it is sometimes dismissed with a "you wouldn't want to go to that party, anyway."

Through the years, we have begun to see that chronic victimization of students by their peers is a significant issue in American schools. Of greatest concern, repeated victimization is a stealthy and treacherous time-bomb that can produce potentially debilitating effects, including increased anger and depression, low self esteem, social withdrawal, and possible suicide.

Numerous studies have shown that peer victimization is associated with psychological distress. These studies go on to state that there are disturbing links between victimization and mental issues, later in life.

For instance, peer victimization in kindergarten predicted later loneliness and school avoidance, and rejection experiences in early adolescence predicted the development of social anxiety and depression. With these types of problems, adjustment becomes much more difficult than it ever should be.

What is the reason for this aggressiveness? What is the reason for bullying? Many girls have no real idea why they become victims, but no matter what the reasoning behind the senseless acts of trauma, the effects of being teased and excluded can be devastating. It has been concluded that social anxiety, social avoidance, loneliness, depression, and general psychological distress are the results of it, though.

Children can develop a distorted sense of proper social relationships, be overly sensitive to negative criticism, and tend to avoid social situations that should be helping to prepare them for their adult lives. In addition, they are more likely to feel they are to blame for their victimization. Victimization is related to poor overall self-concept, as well as to specific identity domains.

These domain areas would include poor physical appearance. Examples of this would be poor physical hygiene, like unbrushed hair, unbrushed teeth, body-odor, not washing properly or often enough, and wearing clothes for longer than appropriately necessary. Because of low self esteem, girls who are victimized by relational aggression tend to have a low opinion of themselves, their appearance, and their worth, so this is projected outwardly in how they take care of themselves.

The domain of romantic appeal can be affected due to many factors. In middle school years, adolescent girls tend to start having their first love interests and crushes, but this can all speed downhill for girls who are experiencing relational aggression. Poor physical appearance can play a role in this, but also, peer ostracization and exclusion causes social development to be inhibited. Note, also, that untrue rumors, broken trust that exposes personal secrets, and peer viciousness can affect a young girl's reputation. This causes their romantic appeal by the opposite sex to spiral downward, effectively driving their self esteem even lower than it already was.

The domain of athletic competence can be hindered because personal motivation is affected when adolescents are going through relational aggression issues. Girls may become lethargic in school activities, like P.E. Sports may not interest them, anymore. Physical activities that were previously enjoyable to them can become a thing of the past. This is all due to the self image and self esteem problems that occur with relational aggression.

Abraham Maslow created a hierarchy of needs that can help explain what victims are experiencing. This hierarchy highlights the needs that are pivotal to the healthy development of young people. When there is an unmet need, their development is hindered, and in some cases, it can be completely halted. Instead of moving to a higher developmental level, they focus their efforts on the unmet need, not by conscious choice but by nature.

Students who are experiencing an unmet need for physical and emotional safety will be unable to focus on higher order needs, such as belonging, self esteem and achievement. This, of course, will cause the other needs to become unmet, which cycles the psychological health of the child further into a downward spiral.

Maslow's work also suggests that students who do not feel emotionally or physically safe won't be able to meet their needs of belonging. It is likely that they will feel isolated and disconnected. Connectedness is the degree to which a person feels she is part of a societal unit and the people associated with said unit. School connectedness, therefore, is the degree to which a student feels that she belongs at, identifies with, and feels an affinity for her school.

Later, we will discuss more about Maslow and his Hierarchy of Needs, which has become a foundational building block to understanding social development at its very core.

7

THE PROFILE OF A BULLY

"A bully is somebody who picks on, and harasses you, and doesn't leave you alone." ~Marlena, age:14

The definition of a bully can be hard to define. The process of bullying is full of intimidation, using superior strength or influence to force peers to do what a girl wants, and using verbal or physical aggression to dominate others. Some would also say that all of this is a way that bullies relieve their own feelings of inadequacy. A bully, as opposed to a child who is generally aggressive, is likely to:

- Target only those children who are perceived to be weaker in some way than them.
- Be unwilling to accept other's ideas.
- Be unwilling to negotiate during play.
- Often oppress or harass others in either a physical or mental way.
- Be of average or above average popularity.

Although many parents and educators may make allowances for children, bullying is a conscious, willful, and deliberately hostile activity that is intended to harm. It induces fear through the threat of further aggression, which creates terror. Whether it is premeditated or seems to be random victimizing, disempowerment is the result for the victimized child.

There are definite components to a bullying situation, which can give us an insight into the seriousness of the situation.

- Imbalance of power: The bully can be older, bigger, stronger, more verbally adept, and higher on the social ladder. They can also be of a different race/ethnicity. This component highlights the superiority that is felt by the bully and the resulting inferiority that the victim feels, in return.
- Intent to harm: The bully means to inflict emotional/physical pain, accepts the action to hurt, and takes pleasure in witnessing the hurt that they are causing their victim.
- Threat of further aggression: Both the bully and the bullied know that the bullying can and probably will occur, again. This is not a one-time event, and when bullying escalates without intervention, a fourth element is added.
- Terror: Bullying is a systematic violence used to intimidate and maintain dominance over someone. Terror struck into the heart of a targeted child is not only a means to an end; it has an end in itself. Once terror is created, the bully can act without fear of retaliation. It becomes a game of cat and mouse.

It has been found that relational aggression is used by bullies in a variety of ways. Some of which are as follows:

- Expression of anger: Relational aggression is a way to express strong negative feelings, particularly when girls don't have the skills to express negative feelings, directly. Instead of finding more appropriate outlets for their anger, they may use others as an outlet.

- Assertion of social dominance: By asserting the power through threatening girls' relationships, a girl can increase her social status, feel powerful, and keep other girls from challenging her position in the social hierarchy.

- Compensation for a lack of self esteem: By excluding others from her clique, a girl can confirm her own sense of belongingness and acceptance.

- Relief from boredom: Girls often report that they use relational aggression to create excitement or drama in their lives.

- Retaliation of jealousy or competition over romantic partners: Girls often use male attention as a way to obtain power. When boys pay attention to another girl, a girl perceives this as a threat to her social standing.

By looking out for these signs and symptoms of relational aggression in the bullies, themselves, parents and educators can identify them and attempt an intervention that will help to redirect them in their aggression and find the problem that is causing the behavior.

8

THE PROFILE OF A VICTIM

"I was pushed and punched by my bully, and I was not allowed to talk to anyone else." ~Monae, age:8

Victims come in all sizes and shapes. They come from all different walks of life, and they are all different from one another. Some are big, some are small, some popular and some are disliked by almost everybody. The one thing that all kids who are bullied have in common is that they are targeted by a bully or bullies. Each one is singled out to be the object of scorn, and thus, they are the recipient of verbal, physical, or relational aggression, merely because he or she was different in some way from those around them.

Over the years, there have been a variety of studies to find out the characteristics of the typical victim. The results agree that victims are most likely:

- Loners who mostly keep to themselves or who have a few friends on the fringe.

- Weak or small or have some physical differences. This could vary to be anything from crooked teeth to a weird haircut.
- Anxious, unassertive, eager to please and quick to concede or give in to others.
- Are socially insecure.
- May have a physical or learning disability.
- May have an overprotective mother, a critical or uninvolved father, or a domineering sibling.

It is important to note that victims are the kind of children parents and teachers love. They are obedient, compliant, constructive, and they try hard to please. Teachers reinforce their behavior because it's so much easier to deal with. They can leave them in their quiet little corner and concentrate on those irritating squeaky wheels.

Those same pleasant traits, though, lead them to be vulnerable and easily influenced. They also may lead them right into the clutches of the schoolyard bully, because as children reach the ages of seven and nine, they become more socially competent, mature and outgoing. The shy little one's sedentary and passive behavior begins to stand out, and this can lead to painful experiences for them.

There are many warning signs of victims of relational aggression, and while most parents do their best to keep the lines of communication open with their children, even the most attentive adults can be unaware of everything that is happening in their child's life. If a child is being victimized, chances are quite good that he or she will never tell an adult.

The following warning signs have been agreed upon for years to help indicate that a child is being victimized:

- Acts reluctant to go to school, shows an abrupt lack of interest in school, or a complete refusal to go.
- Takes an unusual route to go to school.
- Complains of feeling sick and frequently visits the school nurse's office.
- Shows a sudden drop in grades.
- Arrives at home with clothing or possessions that are destroyed or missing.
- Experiences nightmares or difficulty sleeping.
- Acts afraid of meeting new people, trying new things, or exploring new places.
- Refuses to leave the house.
- Waits to get home to use the bathroom.
- Shows increased anger or resentment with no obvious causes.
- Withdraws from family and school activities, wanting to be left alone.
- Is sad, sullen, angry, or scared after receiving a phone call, text message, or email.
- Does something out of character.
- Uses derogatory language when talking about peers.
- Has stopped talking about peers and everyday activities.
- Have physical injuries not consistent with explanation.
- Has stomachaches, headaches, panic attacks, is unable to sleep, sleeps too much, and is exhausted.

Children may not tell an adult that they are being bullied, but they usually give clues. Children can speak as loudly nonverbally as they do verbally. Therefore, it is important to be alert to the frequency, duration, and intensity of any changes in mood or behavior. Bullying can have long-term physical and psychological consequences.

We may ask why the victim doesn't seek help? It has been discussed, a little, but as calm, rational adults, it is hard to understand. How could such unkindness be kept a secret? Why don't children speak up to the adult world?

Unfortunately, this conspiracy of silence is quite common. To youngsters, the idea of tattling is terrifying. Parents and teachers teach that tattling is a bad thing, and although they are only trying to save themselves the time that it would take to deal with minuscule problems, it causes a problem when things are serious.

Parents and teachers may be completely unaware of serious trouble because there is rarely a discussion at home on the subject of bullying. It is difficult for children to discern what problems are big and what are small, so that they can overcome the stigma of the tattletale and tell adults only about important things.

Researchers say parents of both victims and bullies are generally unaware of bullying problems at school and rarely discuss the issue with their children. Sadly, it's often the most badly victimized who report it the least. Often, they are ashamed because they are unable to defend themselves, or because they feel they share some of the guilt for being the object of bullying.

Children have many reasons for not telling adults about these situations. They are ashamed of being bullied. They are afraid of retaliation if they tell an adult. They don't think anyone can or will help them. They have bought into the lie that bullying is a necessary part of growing up. They have learned that "ratting" on a peer is bad, not cool, and "juvenile," even if that peer is bullying them.

It is important to keep a look-out for children who fit this profile, so as to protect them from potentially fatal experiences as a result of bullying and the low self esteem that follows.

9

THE PROFILE OF A BYSTANDER

*"Students just walked by and stared and said things
like, punch her harder." ~Janie, age:16*

Abystander is defined as someone who is present at an event or situation but does not take part in it. Unfortunately, though, bystanders can get sucked into a "mob mentality" that leads them to become supporters who aid and abet the bully through acts of omission and commission. They can stand by or look away, choosing to not become involved in the event but not necessarily doing anything to help, either. They do not come to the aid of their targeted classmates. They can also actively encourage bullying or join in and become one of a bunch of bullies through taking sides with the bully.

The roles of peers in bullying episodes were observed in many urban schools, and studies revealed the following:

- Peers are involved in some capacity with most bullying episodes. Some studies conclude that as many as 80-90 percent of peers have involvement.

- Peers reinforce bullying in most cases. Studies have found that as many as 80 percent of episodes have these types of bystanders that sit by and do nothing.
- Peers are oftentimes more respectful and friendly toward the bullies than the targets.
- Peers are active participants for so many bullying episodes that it is found that as many as 50 percent of episodes have bystanders who, through verbal encouragement for the bully, cheer them on, take their own swipes at the victim, and use name-calling.
- Peer intervention in episodes is so low that many studies conclude that barely over 10 percent have peers coming to a victim's aid or telling an adult about what is going on.

This behavior and lack of motivation to help victims of relational aggression causes questions. Why do so many children who would not personally instigate bullying be so willing to become a part of the attack or turn a blind eye to the plight of the targeted child? This question warrants an answer. There are few valid reasons for this and many excuses, though. Four reasons that come up are:

- The bystander is afraid of getting hurt, themselves.
- The bystander is afraid of becoming a new target for the bully.
- The bystander is afraid of doing something that will only make the situation worse for the victim.
- The bystander does not know what to do.

Because relational aggression is such a detrimental problem for youth, it is important to educate children from a young age on how to handle bullying as a bystander.

10

RELATIONAL AGGRESSION, SOCIETY AND MEDIA

"The adults did not believe my story and accused me of being a trouble-maker." ~Janie, age:16

I n 1902, Charles Horton Cooley introduced a sociological concept called the looking glass self. This concept is unique to humans and has three components:

- We imagine how we must appear to others.
- We imagine the judgment of that appearance.
- We develop our sense of self through the judgment of others.

In the looking glass self, a person views himself or herself through others' perceptions in society and, in turn, gains identity. Identity, or self, is the result of the concept in which we learn to see ourselves as others do. In hypothesizing the framework for the looking glass self, Cooley said "the mind is mental" because "the human mind is social." Beginning as children, humans begin to define themselves within the context of their first social group, which would be their family. Later, they begin defining themselves within society, at large.

It has only been recently, within the last thirty years, that we have begun to speak the distinctive truths of women's lives. The addressing of rape, incest, domestic violence, and women's health has, in the past, been woven under a blanket of silence. Although these issues always existed, over time we have given them a place in our culture by building public awareness, policy, and social awareness.

Unfortunately, though, there is an epidemic of bullying that has also been a hidden culture of female aggression. This epidemic is distinctive and destructive, and it is not marked by the direct physical and verbal behavior that is primarily the province of boys. Our culture refuses to allow open conflict, and it forces females to aggress in nonphysical, indirect, and covert forms.

For the most part, girls are raised to believe that they must be nice girls who heed the advice of their teachers and parents to be polite, patient, and forgiving. They are expected to play in the dramatic play area, pretending to be mothers and wives, while washing dishes, cooking, and sweeping.

Anticipating the reactions of adults, they begin to monitor each other and report good behavior by the ages of seven and eight. However, we live in an aggressive world, and because of this, children witness selfish adults striving for success and power. They see respectable grownups who have merely replaced bullying with their money. Or, they see adults who have replaced bullying with fists for the games of the mind. They see their country's leaders name calling and shouting insults under the guise of criticism. They see the competitive outlook continually reinforced, from the casual card game to the piano recital to the child's classroom.

Children's sense of right and wrong is not yet fully developed, and they cannot understand why society deems it acceptable to engage in war but not acceptable to fight and kill in other instances. Why does one killer go to jail and the other gets a medal? How can we expect our kids not to be bullies when our leaders draw lines in the sand and dare others to cross, pointing out over and over again, that might means right? These are pertinent questions that need answering in order to alleviate relational aggression amongst female children.

Changing attitudes is a difficult task, given that bullies' kick-butt mentality is as pervasive as it is. In fact, that may be part of the problem: the implications of aggression are so prevalent that society has become apathetic to the situation. If it doesn't affect them, personally, it isn't a problem that they should concern themselves with.

And while girls are expected to be quiet about negative feelings, this creates problems when they are faced with situations that are negative. How are they to deal with them? Some deal with the negativity by bullying, and those that are bullied, in extreme cases, deal with it by committing suicide to escape the situation.

For the longest time, it has been believed that women are more caring, nurturing, and relationship oriented than men, but due to recent research and the exposing of the topic of female relational aggression, it is being found that these long-held beliefs are not necessarily the case.

We must ask ourselves why? What is causing it to get so bad?

Many researchers agree that the media has a profound effect on girls. As popular culture and media have evolved, it has opened up a new image of what females should be. It has highlighted huge instances of female violence that is fake and only meant for entertainment, but when presented to young girls, it isn't viewed as such. These constructions of female aggression, manipulativeness, and violence have normalized aggression and positioned girls into a mindset that "this is the way to be."

We have become desensitized to the violence that girls are exposed to on a daily basis. Song lyrics and music videos give covert messages about the acceptability of aggression against women, while newspapers regularly carry stories of overt crimes. Forms of aggression against young women that would be unacceptable in real life are portrayed on television screens every day, after school.

For example, in the move, *Mean Girls*, two cliques of teenage girls become socially aggressive toward each other in school. They plan spiteful tricks and say and write cruel things behind one another's backs. While the movie is a fictional comedy, there is a large degree of truth in the groups' cold-blooded behavior.

This movie, among many others that have presented girls in this type of light, has normalized this type of behavior and caused girls to be accepting of it. It has created a template for girls to fit themselves into, which has changed the old age metaphor of femininity from that of nice to that of meanness.

11

DETAILS ARE IMPORTANT

As Marlena answered the interview questions, she rubbed
Her hands together and put her head down.

R elational aggression is a topic that needs to be presented in a detailed view. Due to the personal and emotional complexity of this book, the design chosen to investigate and examine the issues concerning the victims of relational aggression is based on qualitative research. This research method allows the researcher to build understanding about a social or human problem through exploring distinct methodological traditions of inquiry. It's important to build a complex and interconnected picture by analyzing the words of interviewed persons, reporting detailed views of informants, and conducting the study in a natural setting.

In the research that I have conducted, I've closely examined how relational aggression affects the lives of young girls and will be presenting my findings from their personal perspective. I'll be showing the importance and prevalence of this epidemic of relational aggression, and because of the way I have engaged my participants, they were free to convey their thoughts and feelings as they share their personal stories through dialogues of being victims of relational aggression.

Interviews have been a large part of my research gathering, and it allows researchers to gain insights into others' perspectives about the phenomena under study. It is particularly useful for understanding the respondent's thoughts, perceptions, feelings, and accounts of events.

I chose to use structured interviews, which allowed me to have a predetermined set of questions but to leave open-ended questions that allowed my participants to embellish in their own words. As my understanding grew about the issue of female relational aggression, it helped my question list to evolve, as well.

I also used reflective journaling, which is useful in providing insight into self awareness of behavior, values, assumptions, emotions, and aspirations. Journaling can expose contradictions, misconceptions, and inner conflict. In short, it potentially turns every incident into a potential learning experience, as was the case for some of the participants.

Through the whole process, we will find out many eye-opening answers to questions such as:

- What are common negative feelings and symptoms that victims of relational aggression experience?
- How has relational aggression affected their self esteem?
- What support, if any, did they receive from adults?
- How did they cope? Sports, hobbies, etc?
- How has relational aggression affected their sense of belonging in school?
- How has relational aggression affected their home life?

My participants in this case study consisted of six girls, two Caucasian and four of Hispanic descent. The participants were ages ranging from eight to seventeen years old, and all participants had experience or were at the time experiencing relational aggression. Four of the participants were cheerleaders selected by an owner of a cheer gym. The owner personally counseled these girls through being victimized by relational aggression. The other two participants were selected by my knowledge of them being victims of relational aggression.

My personal research project began in the fall of 2008, and because the participants were minors, the parents were contacted and given an overview of the study, as well as a list of potential questions that their daughters may be asked during the interview. A letter of consent was distributed to each parent. I was available to answer questions and concerns that the parents may have prior to conducting the interviews.

With parental approval, individual interviews were set up with each participant, with the participants choosing the meeting places. Due to the emotional nature of this study, it was important to interview the participants where it was most comfortable for them. All interviews were tape recorded and only available for the researcher and participants to review.

I performed data analysis, which is closely tied to data collection. This is essential to the research process. The aim is to determine key findings and generate theories without fixed preconceptions. A researcher must start with details from fieldwork observations and interviews, allowing them to assemble possible concepts, meanings and relationships. In order to do this, the researcher must be absorbed into this research and the stories the participants share, because it will give a deep view into relational aggression and its harmful effects on young girls.

In the next few chapters, I will present the results of in-depth interviews with six females, ranging in age from eight to seventeen years of age. I'll present a narrative of each girl's experience as it was shared in the interview process. Being sensitive to the nature of the topic, I was careful to give the girls being interviewed the option of not answering the questions, taking a break, or opting out of the interview process. Each of the six girls were willing to participate fully in the process, with some breaks in between for reflection and gathering their composure.

In order to be thorough and detailed, I am including the interview questions:

General Questions:

What is your name? How old are you? What grade are you in? What school do you attend?

Describe What Bullying Means:

What does the word Bullying mean to you; please explain. Describe how you see the person who is bullying you, when she is doing it and after the bullying takes place.

The Cycle of Bullying:

Can you tell me what grade you were in when this started? How long has this been going on? Please describe what the bully does to you. Has it stopped and started again? If it did stop, why did it start again? Was this person ever your friend? How long ago? Do you know why she is doing this to you? Have you asked her why she is doing this? If you have not, why?

The Negative Effects of Bullying:

When this is happening to you how it does make you feel? Can you describe your feelings. How has this affected your self esteem? How has it affected your sense of belonging in the school? Tell me how you feel inside. Sad, or depressed. Can you describe these feelings? Do you ever feel sick? Do you have stomach aches or headaches because of this? Can you describe how you were before this started happening to you?

How Bullying Effects School Life:

When this happens to you, where does it happen? What do other students do about this? Why do you think they do this? Can you describe how you feel when you see this person approaching you? Has this affected your school work? Can you describe how. Have you missed school because of this? If you have, can you describe why. How do you feel in the morning when you are getting ready for school or on the way to school? Have you told an adult at the school? Why did you choose this person? What did they do about it? Did you feel safe after you told? Why or why not. If you have not shared this information anyone at school, why not? Describe your feelings about it.

How Bullying Effects Family Life:

Has this affected you life at home? Please describe how. Has it changed your relationship with your parents/siblings? Have you talked to your parents about this? What did they say to you? How did you feel after talking to them? If you have not, why not? What are your reasons? Why do you feel this way?

Facing the Bully:

If you had the opportunity to talk to this person, what would you say. Explain how you think you would feel about having this chance. How do you think you would feel before, during and after? Explain your feelings emotionally and physically.

Coping Strategies:

How do you cope with the negative feelings of being bullied? Do you have a hobby or a sport that you like to participate in? Is there something that you are good at? How does this help you deal with everything you are going through?

Bringing up such painful memories was a challenge, as I could feel their pain through their narratives. It is important to treat participants with respect, so for the protection and confidentiality of each participant, names have been changed.

12

MONAE'S STORY

"Bullying, to me, is hitting, pushing, telling me to do things that I don't want to." ~Monae, age:8

Monae is an eight year old Hispanic girl who is in third grade and attends a parochial school in California. To Monae, the word "bully" scares her. She defines bullying as, "hitting, pushing, telling someone not to talk to other people, and telling me to do things that I don't want to do."

Monae describes the person who is bullying her as "very mean and selfish." During the time that she is being bullied, she sees her bully as a mean monster. When the bully walks away, Monae sees "a happy monster that got what she wanted."

Monae was bullied off and on for three years. It started in Kindergarten and ended for a while in first grade. Then, it started again in second grade. She was pushed and punched by her bully. She was also not allowed to talk to anyone else. If she did, the bully made her go to the bathroom, where no one could see, and would yell at her and punch her, more. She would also tell her that she wasn't going to be her friend, anymore, and that she would not have any friends, ever. Monae says, "She would punch me really hard on the back."

As Monae explained this, her eyes filled with tears, and so I asked, "Would you like to take a break?" She nodded yes and walked out of the room for a few minutes. She returned after about ten minutes, and we continued the interview.

When asked where the bullying would happen, Monae replied, "In the restroom, at recess on the yard, and in the cafeteria, during lunch. No one saw it happen." She said that no one would see this happening, and that this person was her best friend. She thinks that her friend does this because she doesn't want her playing with anyone else.

When this is happening to Monae, she feels sad. She describes her feelings as feelings like she wants to stop her, but she is afraid of her and what she will do to her. When this is happening to Monae, she says that she does not feel good about herself and that she feels weak, sometimes. She feels sick the night before school, in the morning when she is getting ready for school, and on her way to school. She describes this feeling as a stomachache, feeling nervous in her stomach, and sometimes, headaches.

While Monae talked, she appeared to be getting more upset. She rubbed her hands together as she held back more tears.

Monae says that the bullying happens mostly at recess and lunch time in the restroom, where she is forced to go by her bully. Nobody watches this, and if other girls their age are in there, the girls just ignore it. She does not know why they don't help her.

When Monae sees this person walking toward her, she feels nervous and scared because she doesn't know what she is going to do to her.

Monae says that this has not affected her school work. She has been able to concentrate in class while doing her work and at home while doing her homework. She also says that her grades have not been affected. Monae has not missed school because of this but has tried staying home by telling her mother that she did not feel well.

When Monae is getting ready for school in the morning, she feels nervous. She feels sick with a stomachache and does not want to eat breakfast. On the way to school, she feels nervous and her stomach hurts, especially when she turns the corner and her mother drives into the parking lot. Sometimes, she wants to cry and tell her mother to take her home, but she knows that would not work.

As Monae described this feeling, her eyes started to water, and tears rolled down her face. I handed her a tissue and asked if she needed a break. This time, she said, "No, it's okay. It just makes me feel really sad when I talk about it."

Monae does not feel that this has changed anything with her home life. Although she did share that her older sibling picks on her a lot, she feels protected by her parents when this happens.

In second grade, Monae told her parents about her bully. Her father told her to ignore it. He said that it would get better and that it would go away. Her mother was upset about it and asked her if she could go to school and talk to the teachers and a counselor to ask for help.

When I asked Monae if she agreed to this, she said, "Yes, because I just wanted it to stop. I knew my mom would help me, and I know my mom cares for me." She said that she felt better after she told her mother, and after talking to a school counselor with her bully, she felt safer and not as scared, anymore, because the counselor told her to stop.

Now that Monae is in the third grade, she is not friends with this person, anymore. Monae says, "She still tries to bully me, but I'm not afraid of her, anymore. I know my mom and the counselor won't let her hurt me."

Monae is a cheerleader, and she says that cheerleading makes her feel better about herself because she is happy, there. She has a lot of friends, and she feels safe, there. She also says, "I can do a lot of things that my bully can't do, and that makes me feel a little stronger than her." She feels that the coaches care about her and would never let that happen to her in the gym.

As Monae discussed this, her face glowed, and she smiled as she was talking. She changed her disposition from one of sadness to confidence as she sat up straight in her chair.

13

MARLENA'S STORY

*"Bullying, to me, is somebody who picks on, harasses you
and does not leave you alone." ~Marlena, age:14*

Marlena is a fourteen year old Hispanic girl who is in the ninth grade and attends a public high school in Southern California. The definition of bullying, to her, is "somebody who picks on and harasses you and doesn't leave you alone." Marlena says that when this person is bullying her, she sees a very mean face. After she bullies her, she sees someone who feels satisfied after hurting a person.

When asked when the bullying began, Marlena says that the bullying started in seventh grade and lasted through eighth grade. Since she was on summer vacation, she hasn't seen this person, but Marlena is afraid to start high school, because she knows that she will still have to face her, eventually. Marlena says that her bully pushes her when she sees her, calls her horrible names, like, "tramp, whore, ugly ass bitch, and slut."

As Marlena told me about this, she would not make eye contact, displaying nonverbal signs of discomfort.

Marlena says that this girl was a childhood friend that she grew up with. She does not know why she turned on her or why she picks on her. Marlena says, "Maybe, because she knows I'm sensitive and weak, and I won't do anything about it."

She has not asked the bully why she is doing this to her, because she is afraid to approach her. Marlena says that this girl has a group of new friends who do not like her, and she doesn't know why.

As Marlena described this, she rubbed her hands together and put her head down.

When she is being picked on, she feels sad, afraid, embarrassed, and alone. This has affected her self esteem in a negative way. "I feel bad about myself all the time, and I am ashamed that I can't speak up. Sometimes, I feel like it's my fault, and I don't belong in that school."

Marlena described this feeling with tears in her eyes, and I asked her if she needed a tissue. She shook her head, no, and wiped her tears with the sleeve of her jacket.

Marlena has stomachaches and headache, often, and says that she was a different person before all this started. "I used to laugh, a lot, and act really silly with my friends. I looked forward to meeting up with my friends at school, every day. I was just so happy all the time."

When asked where the aggression usually took place, Marlena answered that the bullying would happen through the school campus, but mostly in the hallways and in the cafeteria, during lunch time. Other students would watch, but no one ever said anything. She said that at times, students would gather around so adults couldn't see what was happening. She would also receive threatening messages on her cell phone. Recalling one message, Marlena said that the bully threatened, "If I see you alone, I'm going to kick your butt."

When Marlena sees this person approaching her, she gets very nervous and scared. She also says, "I just want to hide or run, but I'm embarrassed, so I just let her do whatever she wants to do to me." She says that everyone knows at school, so the students start saying things when they see us approaching each other.

She said that this really affected her school work. "I couldn't concentrate, I was always scared, and I kept hearing her voice in my head, yelling at me and calling me names." She missed a lot of school and would pretend to be sick, but her parents did not believe her. When she was getting ready for school in the morning, she felt a sick feeling in her stomach. On her way to school, say says, "I hate driving to school, every morning, because I feel sick and nervous."

Marlena did not want to tell anyone. She was afraid of making her bully angrier, and she also felt that the teachers would not believe her and that she would probably get in trouble or get kicked out of school. She would try to stay in classrooms with teachers, but they never knew why. She said, "I felt a little safer in the classrooms, but sometimes, the teachers weren't there, and I had to go outside and face her."

Marlena felt that being bullied really affected her family life, as well. She shares, "I never wanted to go anywhere. I was afraid that I would see her, somewhere." She also said, "I became moody and impatient with my little sisters."

Marlena says that she tried to tell her parents, but they just told her, "Walk away. It will stop, soon. Just ignore her." She did not feel better or safer after telling them. At times, she just felt that they did not care.

Noticing the sadness of Marlena, we decided to talk about what makes her feel good. She's a soccer player, and she says that this is how she copes with all her negative feelings about herself and the whole situation. She says, "I love being at practice. I have a lot of friends there that make me feel good about myself, and my coach is very nice and supportive. I know he would never let this happen to me, here. I just wish I could be that strong at school."

As Marlena shared this, she smiles and seemed to find comfort in these thoughts.

If Marlena could tell her bully anything, she would say, "Why did you select me, and why did you break up our friendship? We have known each other for a long time, and I just want things to be the way they were." She feels that approaching her bully would make her feel very nervous, but she thinks she would feel very relieved that she got it off her chest and that they would be friends, again.

14

JESSY'S STORY

*"Bullying is someone who picks on you
and calls you names." ~Jessy, age:12*

Jessy is a twelve year old Hispanic girl who is in sixth grade and attends middle school in California. Jessy attended a parochial school in California from kindergarten to fifth grade, but when her mother lost her job, she had to move Jessy to a public school for sixth grade. Jessy says that this has been a difficult change for her, because she had to leave all her friends behind.

Jessy describes the word bully as "someone who picks on you and calls you names. I see the person who is bullying me as a very mean person. When she is bullying me, I see a mean red face. When she walks away from me, I see a mean red face, but laughing."

When Jessy started her new school, the bullying started. The bullying has been going on for three months. When asked to describe what this person does, Jessy said, "She always gives me dirty looks, calls me horrible names, like bitch, whore, and slut."

As Jessy described this, her eyes filled with tears, and she turned away from me. When I asked if she needed a tissue, she shook her head, no.

Jessy does not really know why she was targeted. She thinks it may be because she is friends with the girl's boyfriend. Jessy says, "This girl used to go with this boy, Aiden, and she thinks I like him, but I don't. He's just nice, and I like talking to him." Jessy says she is afraid to talk to her, and she won't ask her why she's doing this to her.

When this is happening to Jessy, she says, "I feel like I'm not wanted, and I don't belong at that school. I feel depressed." Jessy also says, "I feel depressed, every day, and don't care about anything, not myself, or school, just nothing."

I then asked Jessy, when you say that you are depressed, what do you mean by this? She then answered, "I am sad all the time, and I don't want to do anything. Sometimes, I just stay in my room and cry, a lot."

Jessy says that she has headaches and is always mad. She says, "Before I came to this school, I was always happy, and I had a lot of friends at my other school. We use to dress alike and do other cool stuff, like that. I was just happier."

As Jessy said this, she looked down and started to wipe her tears with her hand. I handed her a tissue. She crumbled it in her hands and continued to look down.

When this girl bullies Jessy, she says it happens before and after school in the hallway, in between classes, and at lunch time. Jessy laments, "When this girl is calling me names, other students hear, even my friends, but everyone just ignores her because they don't want to get involved. My friends tell me, she really hates you." Jessy also says,

"When I see her approaching me, I get really nervous and scared. I don't know what to do. I don't want to hear her calling me names. I hate it."

Jessy says that this has affected her school work. "When I'm doing my work, I start thinking about it, and I can't concentrate. I start thinking, Why am I here? I don't belong here." Jessy says that she always enjoyed school and that at her other school, she always got good grades that she was very proud of. She says, "Now, I get F's in every subject, but I really don't care, anymore."

I asked Jessy whether or not the bully was once a friend, and she said no. Jessy says that when she's getting ready in the morning for school, she feels sick, and she does not want to eat breakfast. She says that she has not told an adult at school, because she doesn't trust any of them. She is afraid that they will not believe her. She also says that she has seen other students try to tell teachers about someone that was picking on them, and the teacher called them a "tattletale."

When Jessy was asked if she had been bullied on the internet, she said yes: "One day, someone sent me a picture of two girls kissing, and I wrote that it was disgusting and gross. The girl who is bullying wrote: all the girls do it, why don't you just suck Aiden's dick!" Jessy says she was embarrassed about what she wrote, and that everyone at school read it, even Aiden! She said, "I didn't want to go to school because I knew that everybody would be talking about it."

Jessy commented on the fact that this and other events have affected her home life in a negative way. "I just like to stay in my room. I don't like to go out anywhere with my family, and I don't like being around a lot of people, like crowds. I was never like that, before." She says that this has changed her relationship with her parents, because she does not want to go out with them, anymore. "They get upset, and when I try to tell them about how I feel about this girl and my new school, they just ask what you do about it. And I really don't know what to say."

When Jessy was asked how she copes with negative feelings of bullying, she said, "I love cheerleading, because it is something that I am good at. I really miss cheer. My mom can't afford to keep me in it, so I don't cheer, anymore, but when I did, I was always happy, there. I had friends, real friends."

If Jessy could face her bully, she would feel very nervous and scared, but she would ask her, "Why do you hate me so much? I never did anything to do. You are making me feel depressed." I asked Jessy, "Do you think this would make you feel better?" She lamented, "No, not really, because I know she won't stop."

15

DANE'S STORY

*"Bullying, to me, is someone who disrespects
and says mean things about people, like about
their height or weight." ~Dane, age:11*

Dane is an eleven and a half year old Caucasian girl who is in seventh grade and attends an intermediate school in California. The definition of a bully, according to Dane, is "someone who is disrespectful and says mean things about people, like about their height or weight. Also, a person who doesn't know right from wrong."

Dane has been bullied by a group of girls since second grade. She says that these girls have been friends with her off and on, and she says, "It will stop and start, again." Dane explains, "They make fun of me because I am smaller and skinnier than them. They call me names like skinny stick and make fun of the hair on my arms."

As Dane was explaining this, she stopped and said, "I feel so good to get this off my chest."

Dane says that the bullying occurred before, after, and during school. It would happen in the hallways, during breaks, at lunch time, and during class. These girls called her names, pushed her, and laughed at her. When asked if any of these girls were ever friends with her, she answered, "Yes, but I don't really talk to them, anymore, because they are mean to me, and it makes me feel sad to think that they were once friends of mine."

Dane says that she has not told any adults at school, but she has told her mother and older sister. I inquired, "What did they say about it? Did they make you feel better?" She says, "Yes, they are very supportive and helpful, especially my sister. She just tells me not to listen to them and that I am better than them. My mom says the same thing, and they both try to make me feel better about myself."

I asked, "How do they make you feel better about yourself?" Dane answers with a confident smile, "They just tell me that I am beautiful just the way I am."

Dane says that many students witness the name calling and pushing, including her friends. When I asked whether anyone helps her when they hear these hurtful names, she replied, "No, nobody wants to start anything with them, so they just ignore them."

Dane puts her head down.

When these girls are bullying Dane, she says, "I don't feel as good as everyone else. I feel really sad and disappointed with myself."

As she said this, she put her head down, took a deep breath, and then continued, "I feel a little depressed, but I just try to be different than them." I asked, "How do you try to be different?" She replied, "Well, I try not to be mean to them, like I just ignored them, but I don't think very bad of them. I actually feel sorry for them."

Dane says that she is always afraid to go into classes because she does not want to be picked on and embarrassed by the mean things they say. She also said, "In the morning, when I am getting ready for school and on my way to school, I feel sick, nervous, and have a stomachache." She also says, "When I'm at school, I hide behind people, so they don't see me." Dane also says that she prefers to stay away from people, because she is afraid to be judged and made fun of.

I asked Dane if this has affected her school work, and she said, "No, not anymore. I am doing much better, now. I don't have much time on my hands to think about all of this. I am very busy with cheerleading and homework. I feel like I have to just stick with it."

Dane also says that she was always silly, friendly, and outgoing. Now, she feels that she is always sensitive. She also says that she just wants to be normal, again. When I ask, "What do you mean by normal?" She said, "Just being myself. Being happy and not always worried about bumping into these girls at school. Always hiding is not very fun. I hate it."

As Dane said this, she became upset, and her eyes filled with tears. She wiped her tears with a jacket that was on her lap. I asked if she needed a tissue, and she shook her head, no.

Seeking to cheer Dane up, I began asking her about her hobbies away from the situation at school. She mentioned her love for cheerleading. Dane is an All Star Cheerleader. She says that cheerleading helps her cope with all the negativity that she faces on a daily basis at school.

Dane says, "When I cheer, I feel so good about myself, because I can do so many things. I have so many friends there, too. My coaches are very supportive, and they always tell me nice things that make me feel good about myself, again."

Dane says that the bullying has not affected her home life. She said, "I am very close to my oldest sister. She is very supportive. She always helps me cope with all of my bad feelings about myself. She tells me not to listen to these girls. My mother also tells me to ignore them. I still feel very close to my family, and I try to just forget about it when I'm home."

She says that if she could tell her bullies anything, she would say: "You are not treating me like a friend. You are not being respectful, and you should just stop this." She says that she would feel very nervous and scared before talking to them and confident, happy, and relieved after she talked to them.

16

JANIE'S STORY

*"Bullying, to me, is someone who is mean and
pushes people up against the wall." ~Janie, age:16*

Janie is a sixteen year old Caucasian girl who is in the eleventh grade and attends high school in California. This is her first year at this school. She has left her last school because of severe bullying. Janie's definition of bullying is, "someone who is mean, and someone who pushes people up against the wall."

Janie says that she was bullied for one year. Janie became upset as tears rolled down her cheeks, as she began to tell me her story.

She said, "These girls pushed me, called me names, pinned me up against the wall and hit me."

As she wiped her tears, I handed her a tissue. She politely thanked me and used it to wipe her tears. She continued on to the interview upon pulling herself together.

She proceeded to tell me about being suspended several times for telling on these girls. The adults did not believe her story and accused her of being a trouble maker. The bullies would actually deny the incidents, creating distrust of the adults that were there for protection. Tearfully, Janie continued telling her story of abuse, stopping intermittently to go to the bathroom.

When Janie returned, she apologized and shared how frustrating it was that nobody believed her situation. I asked Janie whether or not the bullying ever discontinued, and she emphatically replied, "No, it never stopped." As it turned out, one of the girls had been a friend of Janie's, so I wondered if she knew the reason for the dissention. Janie believed it was due to her choosing a different circle of friends. For unknown reasons, the friends were against Janie.

Janie said that the bullying occurred on campus. It happened in the hallways between class, before and after school, and especially at lunch time. She said, "Lunch time was the worst. It was really bad."

Janie's tears rolled down her cheeks, and her face turned red. She took a deep breath. Comforting Janie in this difficult time was difficult. I expressed my appreciation for her willingness to re-live these painful moments.

When asked whether she would like to continue another day, Janie took another deep breath and replied, "No, it's ok."

Janie says that it has changed her very much. She said, "I felt horrible, inside. I was always sad, depressed, and mad." She also said that it was usually about fifteen girls against her. I asked, "Did anyone help when they were hitting you?" She said, "No, the students just walked by or stopped and stared and said things like, punch her harder."

I asked Janie if this affected her school work. She said, "Yes, I would not want to go to school. Every day, when I got up in the morning to get ready, I felt like crap. I felt like I was going to the worst place on earth. I would hold my breath." I asked, "Did you ever tell your parents?" She replied, "No, not at first, because I thought they would not believe me." She went on, saying, "My mom has lost trust in me, because I was always lying to her, saying that I was sick, so she was always upset with me." When Janie admitted to finally telling her mother, her mother was supportive. Janie's mother met with school officials but found it frustrating that they were unreceptive. Her mother finally enrolled her in a new school.

Janie said that coping with all of this was almost impossible. She said, "I would try to ignore them, but it was hard. And even though I had friends, they didn't know how to help me. I felt pretty weak, because I didn't know what to do."

I asked, "Did you have a favorite hobby or sport?" She said, "No, not then, but I cheer now, and I love it. It also helps me feel better about myself."

I asked Janie, "If you could say something to your bullies, what would it be?" She paused for a minute, took a deep breath, and said, "I don't think I could say anything to them." She thought, again, and said, "I would call them low-lifes, and I would ask them why they made people think that I was a bad person." I asked, "How do you think you would feel, inside, before talking to them?" She answered, "angry, scared, and my self esteem would drop because of all the things they said about me."

I asked Janie how she felt about attending a new school. She liked her new school but still felt timid about forming close relationships, so she chooses to talk to the boys more than girls, "because I know they won't be mean to me like the girls were."

17

NICOLE'S STORY

*"Bullying, to me, is someone who is trying to be cool and
getting fun out of hurting me, and someone who is
going to do this, again and again." ~Niclole, age:11*

Nicole is an eleven year old Hispanic girl who attends middle
school in California. She is in the sixth grade. To Nicole, the
word, bully, means teasing, pushing, name calling, and
making fun of someone. Nicole describes the person who is bullying her
as, "someone who is trying to be cool and getting fun out of hurting me,
and someone who is going to do this, again and again."

Nicole says that she was in sixth grade when the bullying started. She
said that it has gone on for about three months. I asked, "What does this
person do to you?" She said, "It's more than just one girl… they make fun
of me and call me names." I asked, "What kind of names?" Nicole put her
head down and said, "Just a lot of mean things, like ugly ass bitch and
stuff like that." I asked, "Do they ever push you?" She replied, "Yes, they
push me, a lot, but it's really one girl that does it. The others just laugh."

Nicole says that one girl always picks on her, but the others have left her alone. She does not know why these girls do this to her. She also says that one of the girls was a friend of hers from kindergarten through fifth grade. She said, "One day, she just stopped being my friend and started hanging around with these girls, and she just didn't talk to me, anymore."

I asked if this girl was the main bully. She said, "No, she just follows along." Nicole says that she never asked the girls why they are doing this to her, because she is too scared to approach them, although she would like to tell them to stop.

I asked Nicole about how all of this bullying makes her feel. She answered, "Sad and mad."

As Nicole said this, her eyes filled with tears. I handed her a tissue. She took the tissue and wiped her eyes. When asked if she would rather discontinue the interview, Nicole said no, she wanted to do it.

I asked Nicole about how the bullying affected her self esteem. She said, "Yes, a little bit. I feel like something is wrong with me." She also admitted to feeling anxious and nervous every day at school. She said, "I have headaches, too."

When reflecting on the days prior to the bullying, she smiled and wished for those happy days.

I asked Nicole where the bullying usually occurs, and she commented that it was usually "in the hallways before, after, and during school." She also said, "During lunch time is when they really bother me." I asked if there are any teachers supervising. She said, "Yes, but they don't really pay attention to everything." She says that when she sees these girls approaching her, she tries to hide.

In the mornings, when Nicole is getting ready for school, she feels nervous, and on her way to school, she has a stomachache. I asked, "Does this affect your school work?" She said, "No, not at all." I asked, "Have you told an adult at school?" She said, "Yes, the principal, because I thought he would do something about it. He told me to ignore it." Nicole does not feel safer after telling adults. I asked if she told her parents. She said, "Yes, but they just said to ignore them, and that is just a thing those girls do."

If Nicole could say anything to her bullies, she said that she would say, "Stop bullying me and just leave me alone!" She says that she would probably be really nervous and scared to approach them, but also thinks she would feel better once she spoke to them.

I asked Nicole how she copes with the negative feelings of being bullied. She said, "I try to just ignore them. I hide from them, so that they don't see me."

I asked Nicole about her favorite pastimes, and she mentioned her love for cheerleading and had lasting friendships in that activity. She also reflected on her hard work and sense of camaraderie with the other cheerleaders.

18

WHAT BULLYING MEANS TO THE VICTIMS

"Bullying, to me, means teasing, pushing, and making fun of someone and name calling." ~Nicole, age:11

A fter carefully reviewing the interviews and my journal writing, I realized that this was a difficult issue for each girl to revisit. I also noticed that each girl was honest and sincere with their stories. They were eager to be heard and also to share their experiences, in hopes to help other girls in this situation. This chapter will reveal the themes and patterns that were presented throughout the interviews.

When each of the girls were asked to describe what the word "bully" or "girl bullying" meant to them, they immediately answered. Each of them describing a mean person with some type of power over them. "A bully is someone who hits, pushes, and tells someone to do something that they don't want to do," according to Monae. Marlena's definition of a bully is "somebody who picks on, harasses you, and just doesn't leave you alone." "A bully is someone who picks on you and calls you names," according to Jessy. Nicole's definition of bullying is "teasing, pushing, making fun of someone and calling them names."

Each of the participants had been bullied by one or more girls. Each of their narratives describe some form of abuse that they suffered on a daily basis, in the hands of a female bully that was sometimes once a friend. As I have explained, before, the whole culture of the bullying epidemic is distinctive and destructive. It hides in the dark, and those who see it happening don't want to get involved. Adults sometimes turn a blind eye, as well, which can make things worse. In all, the victim is left to suffer, internalizing all of it and heading downhill within themselves.

In one of the cases, a participant felt that she was being bullied because of her appearance. Dane describes being called names by a group of girls who chose to be her friend off and on. She felt that she was victimized because she was very skinny and has hairy arms. "They make fun of me because I am smaller and skinnier than them," Dane lamented. Dane describes feeling embarrassed and ashamed. As she described these feelings she looked down to the ground.

Marlena was also called horrible names. She felt that she was targeted because of her sensitive nature and perceived weakness. The bully was also Marlena's best friend in elementary school, so she feels that the bully knows her very well and knows how to hurt her. Likewise, Monae's bully was also her best friend. She thinks that she was targeted because the bully does not want another girl involved in their group.

Jessy does not know why she was targeted. She thinks it may be because she has a friendship with the bully's boyfriend. As Jessy describes this, she looks very frustrated.

Janie's bully was also a best friend of hers in the past. She does not really know why she was bullying her. She said, "One day, she started hanging around with a new group of girls and just changed, and then they all turned against me. I never did anything to them." The pain and confusion shows on Janie's face as she sits slouched in her chair with tears rolling down her face. It is very clear to me that revisiting this experience was difficult for her.

Nicole does not know why she was targeted. When she was asked this question, she shrugged her shoulders and said, "I don't know why they are doing this." Although she did say that one of the bullies in the group was her best friend from kindergarten to fifth grade, she said, "One day, she just stopped being my friend and started hanging around with these girls." Nicole put her head down as she described this to me.

What researchers have found about girls and aggression is more harmful than the physical bullying of the traditional male bully. Instead of targeting a victim, physically, girl bullies attack their victims through what girls value most, which is their friendships and social acceptance. Because girls attack from within friendships and networks of friends, girls tend to protect one another, lying about what is truly going on. This makes aggression harder to identify and intensifies the damage inflicted upon the victim.

It is evident that victims of relational aggression suffer deep emotional and physical effects. Each of the participants reported some type of physical and emotional distress. Each girl stressed that the feeling of anxiety was overwhelming as they were sick with stomachaches, headaches, and fatigue throughout the entire day.

Monae described feeling sad and afraid. She does not feel good about herself, and she feels weak, sometimes. She also suffers from headaches and stomachaches. Marlena says that she feels sad, afraid, embarrassed, and alone. She also feels that it's her fault. When she is getting ready for school in the morning, she feels sick, and nervous.

Jessy describes her feelings as "depressed every day, and I don't care about anything, not myself, school or anything." She also says that she is sad all the time, and does not want to leave her house or be around a lot of people. She suffers from frequent headaches. When Jessy is getting ready for school, she feels sick and nervous.

Similarly, Dane describes her feelings as inadequate and full of disappointment. Janie also shared her feelings, commenting, "I was always sad and mad. I never wanted to go anywhere because I was afraid of seeing these girls somewhere." Nicole described feeling anxious and nervous every day. She also said, "I felt like something was wrong with me." Nicole also has stomach pains in the morning, when getting ready for school, and on the way to school.

This is a trend that is not isolated to my personal participants. It is well-known that children who are frequent victims experience social anxiety, social avoidance, depression, loneliness, and general psychological distress. Many also feel that they are to blame for their victimization, and it is not uncommon for victims to have frequent trips to the nurse's office with complaints of feeling sick. These physical ailments are only the tip of the iceberg. As one looks deeper into the heart and soul of the victims of bullying, it is clear that the pain damages the self esteem.

Throughout the interviews that I conducted, many similarities arose in the way the girls described how bullying has affected their everyday school life. The fear of meeting up with their bully in the hallways, and the anxiety that caused sickness before, during, and after school was powerful. The shame and embarrassment they had to face controlled their thoughts, throughout the day, which severely affected some of their concentration and academic performance.

Monae was bullied in the restroom, at recess, and during lunch in the cafeteria. When she saw the bully walking toward her, she feels nervous and afraid and did not know what to expect from her. Monae did not want to go to school. She felt sick the night before school, in the morning when she is getting ready for school, and when she drove into the parking lot of the school.

Marlena said, "I couldn't concentrate. I was always scared and I kept hearing her voice in my head yelling at me and calling me names." She also said that she missed a lot of school. She would pretend to be sick, so that she could stay home. She also says, "I hated driving to school, every morning, because I feel sick and nervous."

Similarly, Jessy stated that the bullying has affected her school work, and she lacked a sense of belonging. Jessy also admitted that she used to enjoy school and that she always got good grades. Now, she gets F's in every subject, and she doesn't care, anymore.

Janie shared that this had affected her school work very much. "I would not want to go to school, every day. When I got up in the morning, I felt like crap. I felt like I was going to the worst place on earth, and I was always scared. I don't know what to do. I don't want to hear her calling me names. I hate it."

According to so many pieces of research, chronic victimization of students by peers is a significant issue in American schools. Of greatest concern, repeated victimization produces insidious, potentially debilitating effects, including increased anger and depression, low self esteem, and social withdrawal.

How can we help these children, and how can we give our support? We'll talk about this, next.

19

WHAT ABOUT COPING STRATEGIES?

"I'm a soccer player. This is how I cope with all the negative feelings about myself. I love being at practice." ~Marlena, age:14

lthough female relational aggression is such a huge problem in our world, today, there has been little research done on the coping strategies in the specific context of relational aggression. General research, though, suggests that there are two main strategies adolescents use to cope.

- Emotion-Focused Strategies: These include ignoring, withdrawing, and expressing oneself negatively.
- Problem-Focused Strategies: These are characterized by outside support, both social and instrumental, and organized plans of action.

It is important to watch for children who are at risk for relational aggression and to provide therapeutic intervention for them. Besides on-the-spot interventions, some students require additional support beyond what teachers can realistically provide in the classrooms. Students chronically excluded or picked on respond well to group sessions, where they can get emotional support and expand their opportunities for social interactions. Encourage their involvement in activities outside of school, where they can interact with different groups of peers and find possible allies in a world that they might feel lost in.

It has been found that a child's competencies, especially well-developed social, academic, or creative skills, are particularly important to a child's ability to cope. Each of these skills can help the child to deflect or avoid many of the problems she may encounter at school. There are several reasons why competence can more than compensate for emotionally disabling factors that arise with relational aggression.

One of these reasons is self esteem: If children feel confident in any area of their lives, they are better able to put the rest of their live into perspective. They believe, for example, that despite how others might reject or belittle them, they are not a failure, and that despite the voices of despair within them, life is not hopeless. Many strong girls find that much-needed space to grow within creative outlets. There are a variety of ways to find that space.

For example, athletics can be protective because girls in sports are often emotionally healthy. They see their bodies as functional, not decorative. They have developed discipline in the pursuit of excellence. They have learned to win and lose, to cooperate with others, and to handle stress and pressure in healthy ways. They are in a peer group that defines itself by athletic ability, rather than popularity, drug and alcohol abuse, wealth, or appearance.

Another outlet that is protective is an artistic pursuit. These pursuits exercise the mind in a way that allows emotions to channel into whatever is the focus of the creativity. Examples of these pursuits can include writing, reading, drawing, painting, sculpture, singing, playing an instrument, and photography. It would only be limited by the girl's imagination, and that imagination would be pushed to grow and adapt while they learn about how to further excel at their chosen art form. This type of protection will last a lifetime for girls, since there is no peak of excellence to reach in any form of art, and it works well for the shyer girls, since their only true competition is themselves.

The success of coping strategies, though, is influenced by the internal and external resources available to the victim. In the context of victimization, internal resources can include high self esteem, physical strength, intelligence, creativity, and an assertive personality. External resources can include number and quality of friends, the availability of after-school programs, and whether the school has an anti-bullying policy. There is evidence that both sets of resources influence the likelihood of whether or not a victim will continue in their victim status.

There is considerable evidence that many victims lack physical strength, have low self esteem, and are temperamentally unassertive. It has been found that low regard, in combination with behavioral vulnerabilities such as physical weakness and anxiety, contribute to their victimization.

Several studies have linked being a victim to peer rejection, lack of popularity, and having a low quality of friends. Therefore, it is believed that having a good quality of friends, an acceptable number of friends, and having a good general standing in the peer group is a good deterrent from being a victim. Having at least one best friend who reciprocates the friendship and can be trusted is a good deterrent, too.

Adolescents and school age children spend a lot of time away from parents. Their days are filled with school expectations and peer influence. That is why peer groups are the most influential system in which they develop their self esteem. Acceptance in one's peer group can go a long way toward building a sense of competence, particularly in middle childhood, when the frequency of peer contact increases.

Each girl in my interviews had her own way of coping with being a victim of bullying, and each one expressed in many ways, the desperation and loneliness she felt. They shared how they tried to escape the terrible cycle of being victimized on a daily basis. Every girl looked for some type of shield, whether it be from just ignoring the bully, hiding from them, telling someone, or giving all they had left in themselves to an outside activity, which seems like the only thing that saved them from falling apart.

Monae tried to cope with her fear by telling her teachers about this. They told her, "Just ignore it, stop tattle tailing, or just walk away." In turn, she did not feel better after telling these adults. They did not make her feel safer, and she chooses not to tell her teachers, anymore, because she does not want to get into trouble. When Monae told her father, he said to just ignore it. He told her that it would get better and that it would go away.

However, Monae did not give up. She then went to her mother. Her mother spoke to the school counselor about the situation, and the school counselor talked to both Monae and the bully. Eventually, it stopped, and Monae felt safe. Now, Monae ignores the bully.

Another way that Monae copes with the negative feelings of bullying is by cheerleading. She says, "I can do a lot of things that my bully can't do, and that makes me feel stronger and better than her."

Marlena copes with the bullying by staying in classrooms with teachers during lunch time. She said, "I felt a little safer." When Marlena tried to tell her parents, they told her to just ignore her and walk away. Marlena is a soccer player. She says that soccer helps her cope and feel better about herself. She says, "I love being at practice. I have a lot of friends, there, that makes me feel good about myself. I just wish I could be that strong at school."

Jessy admits that this has changed her relationship with her parents, because when she has tried to tell them how she felt about this girl at her new school, they were not comforting.

Jessy's coping strategy was through cheerleading. She said, "I love cheerleading, because it is something that I am good at. I really miss cheerleading. I was always happy, there. I had a lot of friends, real friends."

Dane copes with her negative feelings by talking to her older sister and mom. She also says, "I just try to ignore them, but I don't think very badly of them. I actually feel sorry for them." Dane also copes by hiding from them. She says, "When I'm at school, I hide behind people so they don't see me." Dane is an All Star Cheerleader, and she says that cheerleading helps her cope with all the negativity that she faces on a daily basis at school.

She says, "When I cheer, I feel good about myself, because I can do so many things. I have so many friends, there. I just feel good about myself, again."

Janie says that she was suspended several times for telling on her bullies. She said "Every time I told an adult at school, none believed me. I just stopped telling people at school." She also said that coping with all of this was almost impossible. She said, "I would try to ignore them, but it was hard. Even though I had friends, they didn't know how to help me." Janie said that she didn't have a sport or hobby, then. She is a cheerleader, now. She says that she wishes she was a cheerleader, then, because it has really helped her, a lot.

When Nicole told the principal at her school, he just told her to ignore it. When she told her parents, they said, "Just ignore it, it's just a thing girls do." She also says, "I try to just ignore them. I hide from them so that they don't see me." Nicole is also a cheerleader. She says, "I'm proud of myself when I am at cheer, because it is hard work."

In harmony with the research, the two main strategies girls use to cope are emotion focused strategies, which include ignoring, withdrawing and expressing oneself negatively. They also use problem focused strategies, which are characterized by outside support, both social and instrumental and organizing plans of action. This is what many of the girls interviewed expressed as a means of coping with the aggression.

As we discovered in the interviews, the children's competencies helped them to cope with problems. Some of them had well developed social skills. Some had good academic skills. Some had great athletic skills. Because of these skills and the social integration that they experienced in the peer groups that shared these skills, the girls developed a healthier outlook on life.

Unfortunately, though, our culture is surrounded with myths about bullying. What happens when teachers and parents allow themselves to believe these myths?

Typically, we offer children the usual advice:

- "Ignore them."
- "This happens all the time."
- "They'll move on to someone else, soon"

The subject is, then, considered closed. Parents and teachers move on to "more important" problems or situations, and the child is left to fend for themselves.

When children are told to ignore bullies, this is ineffectual advice that sometimes makes matters worse. The reason for this is because bullies don't simply go away. If they are getting what they want from their victim, whether it is dominance, upsetting the victim, or sport, they are happy and content in their behavior. They do not easily give this up, and most times, it takes an outside influence to put a stop to the aggression.

Our reliance on such generalized comments and attitudes blinds us to the truth of what is actually happening to our children. We fail to listen clearly to what they tell us.

Furthermore, some children may not tell an adult because of stigma against tattling that is persuasive and deep-rooted. It is a taboo that is reinforced in the adult world. Nobody likes a tattletale. Adults and society in general, need to change their attitude towards tattling before children can change theirs, allowing them to speak out against relational aggression.

20

RELATIONAL AGGRESSION AND CYBER BULLYING

"I would receive threatening messages on my cell phone like: If I see you alone, I'm going to kick your butt." ~Marlena, age: 14

Computers and phones have offered girls yet another avenue to communicate with one another and have allowed them to expand their relationships to global proportions. E-mails, instant messages, chat rooms, social media sites, and text messages are now channels through which hurtful interactions can and do occur. Any method of communication that allows for anonymous interaction will change the level of responsibility and accountability a girl feels for her behavior, since it gives her the ability to conceal her identity. It frees aggressors to be crueler and makes victims even more fearful because they don't know their enemies.

Surveys that have been completed in the last ten years for students between grades 4-8 have revealed disturbing information in regards to cyber bullying.

Whether it is in e-mails, instant messing, chat rooms, text messages, or social media sites, children are finding more and more ways to stalk and intimidate their peers. This extends to threats, name-calling, and socially ruining them with pictures, web-pages, and lies that are designed to specifically destroy the victim. Cyber bullies might also use classmates' or friend's PIN numbers and pass codes to send embarrassing e-mails. Sometimes, it is easier to engage in cyber bullying than more direct acts because the bully never personally faces the victim. This form of harassment is also very fast, since an instant message or text message sent at night may spread through an entire school before the first class period.

Despite the fact that girls cannot see one another when they are at the end of a computer or phone, the messages they receive can be as damaging, if not more so than those received in live interactions. Anonymous aggression can leave a girl feeling even more vulnerable and scared than having to face her tormentors.

Nowadays, millions of young people spend hours every day at their computers. They carry around their cell phones like they are attachments of themselves. Cyber bullying involves spreading nasty rumors, gossip, or defamatory information about others, and these electronic outlets allow for them to reach a wide audience while remaining anonymous and undetected.

It's a disturbing thought, but studies have found that about one third of all teenagers who use the internet say they have been targets of a range of annoying and potentially menacing online activities such as receiving threatening messages, having their private emails or text messages forwarded without consent, having an embarrassing picture posted without permission, or having rumors about them spread, online.

Depending on the circumstances, these "Cyber Bullying" or harassing behaviors may be truly threatening, merely annoying, or relatively innocent. However, several patterns are clear. Girls are more likely than boys to be targets, and teens who share their identities and thoughts online are more likely to be targets than are those who lead less active online lives.

When it comes to the question of "Why" teens bully online, it has been found out that in some cases, adolescent cruelty had simply moved from the schoolyard, locker room, bathroom wall and the phone onto the internet. The simplicity of being able to replicate and quickly transmit digital content makes bullying quite easy. All girls have to do is copy and paste the information.

There is a new shocking trend happening, as well. As we have begun to witness in news media, Youtube, and different news articles, camera-wielding attackers, increasingly teen girls, beating a victim so that they can post the videos on popular sites, like Facebook, MySpace, and YouTube. These girls are living in an electronic culture, now, where being in a video makes you famous. Instead of being accountable for their actions and having compassion for others, they see themselves as an actor that is playing a role in their own movie.

There are many differences in cyber bullying versus the traditional schoolyard bullying. Some victims do not know who the bully is, as they hide behind a screen, at times using fake identities to conceal his/her identity. Victims share how hurtful actions go viral in minutes, and a large number of people can be involved in attacks on the victims. Rumors are spread on the internet that everyone can see, and that can affect someone's social life.

It's also easier to be cruel using technology because the bully does not have to see the immediate response of the victim. Some cyber bullies do not realize the harm that they are doing to the person on the other side of the screen or cell phone. Victims are literally humiliated in a worldwide venue which operates twenty-four hours a day.

The combinations of many studies and my interviews have confirmed that victims of Cyber-Bullying suffer a wide variety of negative effects. It is also a fact that there is a strong link between cyber bullying and depression. Unfortunately it is a quiet form of bullying, and the negative effects can go unnoticed, causing detrimental long term emotional effects. Some of the side of effects of cyber bullying include, but are not limited to:

- Anxiety
- Depression
- Loneliness
- Unhappiness
- Poor Sleeping Habits
- Social Anxiety
- Loss of Appetite
- Self-Mutilation
- Suicidal Thoughts
- Loss of Self-Confidence
- Low Self-Esteem
- Loss of Sense of Security
- No Sense of Belonging
- School Absence
- Physical Illness

Like the traditional school yard bullying, cyber bullying also has signs, although many adults do not recognize them. When stress is left unchecked, it can cause severe damage to a child's well being, which can lead to long term social/emotional issues, as well as health issues. Some of the red flags that a child may be a victim of cyber bullying may include, but are not limited to:

- **Social**:
  - Shows signs of aggressive behavior.
  - Unexpectedly stops using the computer.
  - Changes in eating or sleeping habits.
  - No longer wants to participate in things they once enjoyed.
  - Hurts self, attempts or threatens suicide.
  - Appears nervous when receiving text or instant messages.
  - Does not hang out or talk about friends, anymore.
- **Emotional**:
  - Is stressed out or overly anxious.
  - Begins to show signs of depression.
  - Is moody or agitated.
  - Shows signs of aggressive behavior.
  - Withdrawn or shy.
- **Academics**:
  - Drops in grades.
  - Does not want to go to school.
  - Skips school.
  - Loses interest in school.

One of the most noticeable red flag is when a child withdraws from any form of technology. Make sure to talk to the child. They may be a victim of cyber bullying.

Bullying has entered the digital age, and although the impulses behind it are the same, the effect is magnified. In the past, materials of bullying would have been whispered, shouted or passed around. Now, with a few clicks, a photo, video or conversation can be shared with hundreds via email or millions through a website, online profile or blog posting.

21

BRINGING CYBER BULLYING INTO THE LIGHT

"When things are said about you, online, everyone can see it, and it can ruin your reputation." ~Nikki, age:13

Cyber bullying is a new form of bullying that has taken the world of technology by storm. Like traditional bullying, it is destroying the lives of our youth, every day. Studies show that girls are more likely than boys to engage in this form of bullying, which also makes this another form of relational Aggression. To enlighten my readers on this topic, I decided to continue with the qualitative research method, as stated in Chapter 12. I chose to interview 3 girls who are victims of cyber bullying. The girls ranged from age 12-15.

Again, using the interview process and reflective journaling helped me to better understand, first hand, the horrible effects of cyber bullying. After in depth research into this horrible trend, I came up with questions that would help us understand how cyber bullying affects the lives of girls. Through the interviews that you will read in the next section, you will find out many shocking and disturbing answers to questions such as:

- What each participant things the word cyber bully means.

- What cyber bullies actually do, online, to torment their victims.

- Common negative feelings and symptoms that victims of cyber bullying experience.

- How cyber bullying has affected their home and school life.

- If the participant could face the cyber bully, what would she say?

- How has cyber bullying affected the participant's sense of safety, belonging, and self esteem?

- How has cyber bullying affected the participant's academic success?

- How has cyber bullying ruined the participant's reputation, at school?

My participants, in this case study, consisted of three girls, two of Hispanic decent and one Cuban. The participants were of the ages ranging from twelve to fifteen years old, and all of the participants are currently experiencing cyber bullying. All three girls were selected from my knowledge of them being victims of cyber bullying through conversations with their parents.

With parental approval, individual interviews were set up with each participant. All interviews were conducted in the comfort of their own home. Each parent provided a quiet place to sit.

In the next few chapters, I will present the results of the in depth interviews of the three girls. I will present a narrative of each girl's experience that was shared with me. With such a sensitive and painful topic, I was sure to began the interview with letting each girl know that they did not have to answer every question, unless they wanted to. Each of the three girls were willing to fully participate, all wanting to help shed the light on this awful trend.

To be thorough and detailed, I am including the interview questions:

General Questions:

What is your full name? How old are you? What grade are you in? What school do you attend?

Describe What Bullying Means:

What does the word bullying mean to you; please explain. Describe how you see the person who is bullying you, when she is doing it and after the bullying takes place.

Describe What Cyber Bullying Means:

What does the word cyber bullying mean to you?

The Cycle of Cyber Bullying:

What grade were you in when the cyber bullying began? How long has it been going on? Please describe what the bully has done to you on-line. Has it stopped and started again? If it did stop, why did it start again? Was this person ever your friend? How long ago? Do you know why she is doing this to you? Have you asked her why she is doing this to you? If you have not, why?

The Negative Effects of Cyber Bullying:

When this is happening to you, how does it make you feel? Can you describe your feelings. How has this affected your self esteem? How has it affected your sense of belonging at school? Tell me how you feel inside? Sad or depressed. Can you describe these feelings? Do you ever feel sick? Do you have stomachaches or headaches because of this? Can you describe how you were before this started.

How Has Cyber Bullying Effected Your School Life:

Has cyber bullying effected your school life? Can you explain how? Have you lost interest in school? Have your grades dropped? How do you feel when you are at school?

How Has Cyber Bullying Effected Your Home Life:

Has this affected your home life? Please describe how. Has it changed your relationship with your parents/siblings? Have you talked to your parents about this? What did they say to you? How did you feel after talking to them? If you have not, why not? What are your reasons? Why do you feel this way?

Facing the Bully:

If you had the opportunity to talk to this person, what would you say? Explain how you would feel about having this chance? How do you think you would feel before, during and after? Explain your emotions.

Coping Strategies:

How do you cope with the negative effects of being bullied? Do you have a hobby or sport that you like to participate in? Is there something that you are good at? How does this help you deal with everything that you are going through?

Having each girl talk about their painful experience was a challenge, as I could feel their pain through their narratives and disposition. It is critical to treat each individual story with respect and compassion, so for the protection and confidentiality of each participant, names have been changed.

22

COURTNEY'S STORY

"The word, cyber bullying, means to be bullied, online, where the bully feels more confident, because it's not face to face." ~Courtney, age:15

Courtney is a fifteen year old Hispanic girl who is in tenth grade and attends high school in California. Courtney defines the word bully as threatening and negative. She also says that a person who bullies is mean and thinks they can just get their way. She describes the person who is bullying her as a monster.

Courtney defines the word cyber bullying as a person who bullies, but online and through texting. She feels that through cyber bullying, the bully is more confident, because they are behind a screen or phone, instead of being face to face.

Courtney has been cyber bullied for one year, now. She says that it has been consistent and has not stopped. The cyber bully created two hate pages of Courtney on a popular social media site. One page is still active and visible, while the other was deleted after two weeks. As Courtney sit curled up on her sofa, her voice very low, she began to tell me what was said on these pages.

The look on Courtney's face spoke louder than her words; this was a very difficult topic to talk about. I made sure to tell her that she did not have to answer the question, but she said she was fine and wanted to proceed. Courtney said that pictures of her were put up on a page. She was called names such as, bitch, slut, ugly and other names she did not want to repeat. She was also accused of "talking" to multiple boys. Courtney also said that there were several people who joined in on the attack.

The cyber bully attends the same school as Courtney, so she also sees her on campus. I asked if this person was ever her friend, she said yes. Courtney does not know why she is doing this to her. Courtney says that they were friends since middle school, and all of a sudden, she just turned on her. Courtney never asked why she is doing this to her. She said she just didn't want to bother.

When the cyber bullying is happening to Courtney, she feels sad and depressed. She also felt that her self esteem was affected, because she actually started thinking it was her fault and started questioning herself. She felt stressed, all day long, and had frequent stomachaches.

Courtney says that she was very outgoing, happy and confident before all of this happened. "I looked forward to being at school," she said.

Courtney feels that this has affected her school life. She feels nervous when she is on her way to school and when she arrives. She dreads seeing this person at school. When she sees this person, she tries to avoid her, but this person just stares at her and says things about her in groups of friends, making Courtney feel very uncomfortable.

Courtney also says that she feels humiliated and embarrassed about the things that are said about her online, and she feels that everyone is staring at her and talking about her. Although this has effected how she feels at school, it has not affected her grades. Courtney maintains a 4.0 grade point average.

Courtney says that being a victim of cyber bullying has affected her home life, especially with her younger sibling. She has less patience and does not want to spend time with her anymore. She also says that she just wants to stay home and not go anywhere or do anything. Courtney says that she did not want to tell her parents, but when she finally told them, she felt relieved, and it brought them closer together. She also says that it was hard to see how much the whole incident has hurt her mother.

If Courtney could face this person she would ask her "Why are you doing this to me? You use to be my best friend." She says that she would feel scared and nervous about approaching her, but would feel better if she talked to her and it just stopped.

Courtney copes with the negative effects of cyber bullying by talking to her friends about it, and she is a cheerleader at her school. Cheerleading helps her with her confidence and self esteem. As Courtney shared this, she smiled and changed her disposition.

23

NICHOLE'S STORY

*"Cyber Bullying means being embarrassed, online, feeling helpless
And worthless and tears you down." ~Nichole, age:13*

Nichole is a thirteen year old girl of Cuban decent. She is in eighth grade and attends a parochial school in California. To Nichole, the word bully means putting others down, making people feel worthless, making a person feel like they don't belong. It is someone who finds it funny to hurt people and doesn't care about how they hurt others. Bullies think hurting others is funny and laugh about it with their friends.

Nichole describes cyber bullying as being embarrassed, online. It is feeling helpless and worthless. She also states that cyber bullying can tear a person down, and it's horrible how a group of people will attack someone through social media sites where everyone can see it, and it can ruin a person's reputation at school.

Nichole has been cyber bullied consistently for one year. It started in seventh grade and has continued to now, into the eighth grade. The cyber bullying happens mostly on the popular social media sites. Nichole explains that the cyber bully makes fun of her constantly, online. The bully makes fun of how she looks, how she dresses, and constantly judges her. The cyber bullying will start with one person, and then, different people join the attack.

As Nichole explained this, she showed signs of distress by moving in her chair, rubbing her hands together, and constantly touching her face. I asked her if she needed a break, but she said she was fine and continued. Nicole went on with the interview, continuing with what the bully does online. The bully calls Nicole names such as, fake, slut, whore, attention-whore, trying too hard, a wannabe, fat, and bitch.

Nicole says that when school is out on holidays or vacations, the cyber bullying is worse and more often. She says that she has been in the same school with the bullies since kindergarten, and they were all friends. She does not know why this is happening or why she is a victim of cyber bullying.

Nicole suffers many side effects from cyber bullying. She is afraid to be by herself, always feeling that people are watching her. She says she often feels depressed, all alone, and feels like she will never be good enough. Nicole started to believe that she was everything that they were saying about her. She felt like she was losing her identity.

As time went on, she began to lose trust in people and always had a guard up. Nicole also says that she used to be very confident, and now, her self esteem is dropping. She felt like she did not have a sense of belonging, because everyone would gang up on her during online bullying.

Nichole shared that she always has a stomachache and frequently vomits. She has chronic headaches, and sometimes cries, all day. Nichole says that before all of the cyber bullying began, she had an almost perfect life. She had so many friends.

Nichole says that her school life was affected by feeling that she didn't belong there. She kept thinking "Why am I here? I don't belong here!" she felt like no one at school cared about how she was feeling. She was confused and just didn't want to go to school. When she was at school, she could not concentrate.

Nicole feels that her home life was also affected. She is depressed, a lot, and wants to just stay in bed, all day. "I could not get up and did not want to go out," she told me. She also felt like her relationship with her mother was changing. They were always close, and now, they were becoming distant, because Nichole was always angry and sad. She felt like she did not know how to release it. She also shared that she was mean to her younger brothers. They used to be very close, and now, they are not. She just prefers to stay away from everyone and stay in her room.

Nichole was hesitant on telling her mother about the cyber bullying. When she did tell her mother, she was very sad and hurt, but Nichole said that she felt a little better, but she still holds a lot in.

If Nichole could face the bullies, she would tell them that what they are doing is not cool, it may seem funny, but it's not! They don't know how much they can really hurt someone. Nichole thinks that she would feel relieved and proud of herself for confronting them.

Nichole copes with the negative effects of cyber bullying in different ways. She listens to music, reads, eats a lot, watches television and talks to her friends and her mom. She also plays soccer and dances.

Nichole admitted to cutting herself as a way of coping with the horrible pain she was feeling. When telling me this, she looked down and avoided eye contact.

24

CELESTE'S STORY

*"Cyber Bullying means when people call you names
And make fun of you, online." ~Celeste, age:13*

Celeste is a thirteen year old Hispanic girl who is in eighth grade. She attends a public middle school in California. To Celeste, the word bullying means when people call you names and just being mean to someone. Celeste feels that cyber bullying is the same as bullying, with the only difference being that it's on social media sites.

Celeste says that she was cyber bullied consistently for one year, from age twelve to thirteen. She says that a "hate page" was created of her on a popular social media site. The cyber bully posted daily pictures of Celeste. As she explained this, she kept her hands clasped in between her knees.

Along with the pictures, the cyber bully said horrible things to Celeste. Things that were said included, you are too skinny and ugly. Celeste's disposition changed as she looked down and continued. The cyber bully also said that Celeste is too skinny, she is anorexic, she looks like a stick, and she needs to eat more. Celeste said that other people would also go on the hate page and comment, making fun of her. The page of Celeste is still up.

When Celeste was asked if this person was ever her friend, she said yes. They were friends in elementary school. Celeste does not know why she is doing this to her, and she has not asked her why.

When Celeste sees the pictures and comments on the hate page that was created of her, she feels sad. She feels depressed and doesn't want to do anything or go anywhere. She just wants to stay in bed, all day. Celeste says that she always had a stomachache and loss of appetite.

Celeste feels that her school life was affected. Her grades went down, because she just stopped trying. She felt like she couldn't concentrate, and she just kept thinking about all the names that she was being called and how she was made fun of. She felt humiliated and embarrassed. She felt like, when it came to school, she didn't want to do anything.

Celeste also feels that it affected her home life by her not really having patience with her siblings and always feeling angry and not knowing how to deal with all the negative feelings.

Celeste did tell her mother about the cyber bullying, and her mother told her not to worry about it, that she was beautiful, and not to let people get to her. Celeste felt better after telling her mother, and she says that she felt relieved. Celeste did not tell any teacher or staff at her school. She does not feel that they would do anything to protect her.

If Celeste could face her bully, she would ask her why she is doing this to her. She would also let her know that she is hurting her. Celeste thinks that before approaching the bully she would feel very nervous, but afterwards she would feel like she released a ton of bricks and stress.

When I asked Celeste how she coped with the negative feelings of cyber bullying, she said that she talks to the people that are her friends. She also said that if she could talk to girls that are going through cyber bullying, she would tell them to stay strong and not to let anyone tell you different, just be who you want to be!

25

CYBER BULLYING AND NEGATIVE EFFECTS

"It isn't simply a matter of ignoring the bullying or getting over it... because as you are building your image of yourself, others play such a powerful role in helping you do so. Bullies create such a negative image of you that it's hard to feel positive about yourself while it is happening." ~Selina Lamken

Through my research and interviews, it is evident to me that cyber bullying has horrible effects on the victims. Although it was difficult for each of the participants, they all agreed to want to help me bring the negative effects of this new epidemic into the light. I appreciated each girls' story as they each sat nervously in their chair and shared such a painful part of their teenage life with me.

When I asked each girl what cyber bullying meant to them, they paused to really think about the difference between bullying and cyber bullying. They each had their own description of cyber bullying, although they were each similar in many ways.

To Courtney, cyber bullying involves a person who bullies, but online and through texting. She also feels that through cyber bullying, the bully is more confident because they are behind a screen. Nicole describes cyber bullying as a person being embarrassed, online, making them feel helpless and worthless. She also feels that cyber bullying can tear a person down. Celeste says that cyber bullying is when people call you names and make fun of you, online.

Each of the girls were cyber bullied consistently and are still victims. Each said that the cyber bullying was started by one person, but eventually, more people joined in on the attacks. Two of the three girls were humiliated online with "hate pages" that were created of them by the cyber bully. Pictures were posted of them and each were called horrible names. The other victim was also called horrible names, but it happened on her social media site. Each girl shared that the cyber bully was once a close friend of theirs, and they did not know why this friend turned on them. Each girl was hesitant to tell their parents, but eventually did. Through their stories, it seemed that each of them received positive support from their parents.

Another important issue that arose was that each parent was deeply hurt to find out that their child was being humiliated, online. After each interview, each parent was also eager to be heard. They each expressed their anger, hurt, and frustration that school staff was not supportive of this type of bullying. One parent even went as far as getting the police department involved, but even there, there was there no support. I was enraged to hear that parents were getting the runaround and no peace, whatsoever, was given. Instead, there were sleepless nights, fear, anxiety and depression. No help!

Behind each girl was also a list of painful side effects of cyber bullying. It was startling to me that all of their symptoms were similar. Each complaining of depression, loneliness, humiliation, intimidation, loss of identity, loss of safety and sense of belonging, stomachaches, headaches, anxiety, fear, stress, change in appetite, and change in sleeping patterns. It was very painful to hear each of them describe these devastating feeling to me. I could not only hear it in their voice, but see it in their eyes. Everything that they described to me was robbing them from the teenage life that they so deserve. Instead, they are being haunted, every day, by the horrible effects of cyber bullying.

Through my interviews, it was evident that cyber bullying severely affected the school life of each girl. Courtney felt nervous on her way to school. She feels humiliated and embarrassed when she is at school, thinking that everyone is starring at her. Nichole felt like she did not belong, and she felt like no one at school cared about how she was feeling. Celeste says that her grades dropped, because she didn't care, anymore. She felt like she could not concentrate, because she kept thinking about the names that she was being called. Each girl felt humiliated because of the pictures and words that were exposed online and how many people were seeing this. They all felt that their reputation and sense of identity was destroyed.

The thought that each girl's school days are spent in darkness and sadness, desperation and loss, instead of joy, excitement and anticipation of what middle school and high school should be, saddens me and leads me to believe that the school systems are not doing what they should be to protect these young girls.

Each of the girls also shared that their family life was somehow affected. Courtney, Nichole and Celeste each described how they did not want to go anywhere. They just wanted to stay home and in bed, all day. Each girl discussed having siblings and how they took their anger and frustrations out on them. Courtney, Nichole and Celeste said that they lost patience, energy, and motivation for their siblings. They each felt that they had no interest in being around their siblings, whereas before, they did.

All three of the girls would like to face their cyber bully/bullies and ask them why they are doing this, but they each said that they prefer not to approach this person. They each expressed the feeling of anxiety every time they see them on campus, so approaching them would not be something they would do. Although this is the case, they all felt that they would feel relieved if they did let it out to express their hurt, anger and frustrations.

Coping strategies for each girl was different. Music, television, dancing, talking to best friends, eating, sleeping, and sports were all ways of coping. The one who stood out to me and left an impression in my heart was Nichole, who unfortunately turned to self mutilation. Cutting, although for a short time, was just painful to hear and see. This is unacceptable! No young girl should feel that she needs to release pain through pain. This is alarming and frightening! Through my research, I found that many teenagers turn to some type of self pain.

We must open our eyes and minds to this type of bullying. We must learn to read the signs. We must step away from our busy lives and observe, listen, and learn from our children. Chances are, if your child or any child is a victim of cyber bullying, it is only a matter of time before they are stripped from living... and the failure to thrive will surly sink in.

26

TYING IT ALL TOGETHER

"What is necessary to change a person is to change his awareness of himself." ~Abraham Maslow

Although Abraham Maslow introduced his concept of the Hierarchy of Needs in the 1940's, it still lives up to its rationale, today. It helps us to better understand our basic needs of life, from our physiological needs, to our sense of safety, to our sense of belonging, esteem, and finally, our self actualization. In order for one to thrive, it is essential that all of these needs are met.

I am a firm believer of Maslow's Hierarchy of Human Needs. My research and interviews have convinced me that it is critical for every child to have their sense of safety and belonging needs met. Without this, it would be very difficult to reach a high self esteem, and eventually, self actualization, the realization or fulfillment of one's talents and potentials, and the feeling of ultimate achievement in life.

After my in-depth research and interviews, I quietly reflected on all of the negative effects bullying and relational aggression has on the lives of our youth. It saddens me to know that many of these girls, at such a young age, had no sense of safety or belonging in a place where they were sent to learn, which led to negative self esteem and self image. Their words of pain, loneliness, and desperation echoed through my heart as I wrote this book. My purpose for writing this book is to enlighten you, the reader, on this horrible epidemic that is infecting our youth.

So, in order to understand the imbalance that occurs inside an individual whom is a victim of relational aggression, we will look at the individual sections of Maslow's Hierarchy of Needs.

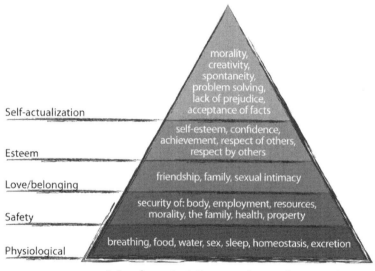

Maslow's Hierarchy of Needs

Physiological Needs - According to Maslow, our physiological needs consist of things such as water, air, shelter, food, sleep, intimacy and human touch, as well as what is presented on the chart. Victims of bullying may have some of their physiological needs met, but are deprived of a few.

Sleep, for instance, could be an unmet need. Because of chronic anxiety, stress and fear, victims lack one of the main ingredients to a healthy life: sleep. Without proper rest, it is difficult for someone to learn or focus in class and carry out everyday functions in life. At times, the girls that I interviewed looked stressed, exhausted, and disorientated.

Another important factor of physiological needs is intimacy and touch. Girls hold friendships very dear to them, and without close intimate friendships, girls do not thrive. Young and adolescent girls find friends to be as important to them as the air they breathe, the water they drink, and the food they eat. They are dependent on one another, and when this is threatened, so is the wellbeing of a girl.

Safety Needs – These include needs for safety and security, both physically and emotionally. Security needs are important for survival, but they are not as demanding as the physiological needs. Examples of security needs include a desire for steady employment, health care, safe neighborhoods and schools, and shelter from the environment.

When girls are being victimized, their sense of safety is jeopardized. My research and interviews reinforced that victims of bullying suffer a great deal of health issues which affect their sense of safety, such as abdominal pain, headaches, insecurity and depression. In the words of one young girl through my research, "Friends are like security blankets when everything is changing."

The sense of safety is critical for girls while growing up. It is a proven fact that if a child does not feel safe in their environment (classroom/school), it is difficult to learn. Children who do not feel physically or emotionally safe will not be able to meet their need for belonging.

Belonging Needs - Maslow describes this step as belonging, love and affection. It's where relationships such as friendships, romantic attachments, and family will help satisfy this need. Girls thrive on acceptance from peers, belonging in social groups, and being part of a clique. Belonging is the feeling of connectedness. Connectedness is when a person feels that he or she is part of a social group or unit and everyone associated with it. Feeling connected to school life gives a child the sense of belonging.

When studying Maslow's Hierarchy and the sense of belonging, it indicates that students who are being mistreated at school have less confidence, which causes them to be more vulnerable to negative influences, self destructive behaviors, and low self esteem.

Through the interviews, the girls spoke of feeling disconnected, depressed, lonely, and isolated. In the words of one girl, "I feel bad about myself, all the time, and I am ashamed that I can't speak up. Sometimes, I feel like it's my fault, and I don't belong in school." From another girl, "I feel like I'm not wanted and don't belong at school. I feel depressed, every day, and don't care about anything, not myself, school, just nothing."

These are testimonies that bullying and relational aggression can and will destroy the sense of belonging for any child. Without a healthy sense of belonging, there is no way a child will have a strong, positive sense of self, which leads to self esteem.

Self Esteem Needs - After the first three needs have been met, esteem needs becomes ever more important. These include the need for things that mirror on self esteem, personal worth, social recognition, and accomplishment. What lives in my mind is the disposition of the girls that I interviewed. They were so fragile, insecure, and sad. Their body language spoke to me before their words did, as each sat slouched in their chair. They had very little eye contact, they looked down to the ground, rubbed their hands together, squeezed a jacket or sweater in hand; all with tears rolling down their cheeks as they were crying. This was definitely the most difficult part of the interviews. It was evident to me that being bullied had destroyed every ounce of self esteem and self worth that these girls had. It was a painful reminder of seeing my own girls going though the horrible side effects of bullying and relational aggression.

According to Maslow, a self actualized person is autonomous and independent. They have a solid view of reality and are accepting of themselves, others, and the world around them. They are able to cope with stressors in their life. A self actualized person is able to establish meaningful relationships with less people rather than fake bonds with many people. They are able to function in everyday living with no problem.

When a child lacks the sense of safety, belonging and self esteem, it is almost impossible to be self actualized.

A person who does not meet self actualization and the feelings of accomplishment will struggle in everyday life with school, work and relationships. My research and interviews have proven this. After reconnecting with a few of the girls I interviewed, I was convinced that this is evident as a few struggled through the rest of school, getting kicked out of school, not having the desire to go to college, find a job, and struggle with identity and relationships.

This just saddens me that there are many victims out there at the hands of a bully every day, struggling and being stripped of their happiness, wholeness and sense of well being. This will eventually destroy our future women, sisters, daughters, wives, mothers, friends and professionals. We must put a stop to this horrible epidemic.

27

REINFORCED THOUGHTS

*Participants' responses indicate that being a victim of bullying has
taken away their sense of belonging, safety and self esteem.*
~Yvette Michelle Apodaca

'

The data that I collected reinforced my own perception of the multiple forms of trauma that children go through in forms of relational aggression. These include ones that are subtle and not obvious to significant others, such as being alienated, ostracized, and rejected by peers.

My research shows that it can affect every aspect of a child's life. Relational aggression affects important key aspects of their development, such as their physical and emotional well-being, participation in family life, sense of safety and belonging, and academic performance. Relational aggression robs girls of growing up in a normal manner and living a normal life.

Participants' responses indicate that being a victim of bullying has taken away their sense of belonging, safety, and self esteem. It has literally diminished their will to thrive during a critical period in their lives. Many researchers agree that girls need the comfort of belonging and friendships that are healthy.

My research has also proven that without friendships and peer relations, their cognitive, social and moral development will be diminished, as well as psychosocial adjustment and socio-emotional well-being. It is also evident, through my research and interviews, that young girls who suffer from relational aggression lose their sense of identity and self worth, which can have a negative impact on their entire outlook on themselves and life.

Compared to other forms of aggression, such as physical violence, relational aggression is quieter, more insidious, and harder to detect.

Although this form of aggression is ignored, my research has proven that it is far more painful to the victims than physical abuse, because the victim continues to be eaten away from the humiliation, fear, isolation and emotional exhaustion that they endure every day at the hands of their tormentor.

What was disturbing to me is that "girl fighting" is almost accepted by saying "It's just a thing girls do." So, administrators, teachers, and parents cover their eyes to this form of abuse, not realizing the harmful effects until it is too late.

What was most shocking to me was the ignorance and denial of this phenomenon among adults who turned their cheek the other way. I was astounded to hear the participants say that they had no support from administration and staff at their schools. Although many schools stress that they have zero tolerance for bullying, after listening to the participants' responses, this policy seems to have fallen short for victims of relational aggression.

When Monae tried telling a teacher about being bullied, she was told, "Just ignore it, stop tattling, walk away." She did not feel safer. She felt alienated by this response. In fact, she chose not to tell a teacher, anymore, because she did not want to get in trouble.

Marlena felt that the teachers would not believe her and that she would get in trouble. Similarly, Jessy does not trust any adults at school. She also remembers seeing a student get in trouble for telling on someone. He was called a tattletale at school, by the teacher!

Speaking to the lack of support, Janie's experience of being suspended several times for telling on her group of bullies was consistent with the lack of adult support. When Nicole told the principal, he told her "Just ignore it, it's just a thing girls do."

It was obvious that each of these girls were calling out for help. The message that they received from adults was: "we cannot help you." This left each girl feeling stranded, with no place to turn for help, with broken trust, and deeper feelings of anxiety and desperation. Help was not there.

Ultimately, all of this would lead to a lower self esteem, causing each girl to feel that no one cares about them, so why should they care? Furthermore, by putting the victim aside, adults are reinforcing one of the characteristics that make her vulnerable in the first place: isolation.

A victim is a victim because she is left alone.

It was also surprising to hear that even parents were not supportive or helpful. Most responded to their child's plea for help by saying things such as, "Ignore it, walk away." Once again, each participant's distress was overlooked. When Monae told her father about being bullied, he brushed it off saying, "Just ignore her, it will stop, soon."

Marlena's parents told her the same thing, "ignore them, walk away." When Jessy told her parents, they told her, "So, what do you do about it?" Nicole says that when she finally told her parents they said, "Ignore it, and it's just a thing girls do."

Telling a child to 'walk away' does not work, because bullies tend to target their victims in places that corner them. They relentlessly push, both mentally and physically, to get what they want from them, and walking away is a sign that the victim is attempting to take away what the bully wants. At this point, it is likely that the bully will turn physically aggressive to get what they want, instead of relying on mental means.

I felt each girls' desperation and feeling of loneliness as they shared this information. Being turned away by teachers is one thing, but being turned away by a parent seems to be even harder on the child.

As a parent of young girls who battled with relational aggression, I felt a great interest in understanding this growing phenomenon. What was startling to me is that this research has left many unanswered questions.

What does this say about our schools and society?

Parents and teachers must acknowledge this horrible epidemic. They must take steps to help these children. There is a need to look closer. There is a need for parents and teachers to become aware of this quiet, yet damaging type of bullying.

The process of writing this book has been an amazing experience for me. Through this journey, I have not only learned how to help my own daughters, but the many daughters that suffer from being victims at the hands of bullies, every day of their lives. And most importantly, I feel that this research has helped me become a valuable resource for parents and teachers.

Writing this book was difficult as I sat and listened to each participant explain the fear, loneliness, humiliation, and pain that they have had to endure as victims of relational aggression. They go from having friends one minute to having no friends, at all, and the thought of these girls being so afraid of going to school that it literally caused mental and physical illness saddens me. It was a painful reminder of how I watched my own children go through this, although I never imagined the devastating consequences they must have suffered. And from the responses, I don't think any parent or teacher realizes the negative consequences that girls suffer from relational aggression.

According to Abraham Maslow's work, students who do not feel emotionally or physically safe won't be able to meet their needs of belonging. It is likely that they will feel isolated and disconnected.

I am a firm believer in Abraham Maslow's theory. It is evident, through my findings, that when children have an unmet need, they focus on that unmet need, not by conscious choice, but by nature. When their physical and emotional safety is unmet, they will not be able to focus on higher-order needs, such as belonging, self esteem, or achievement. Thus they become careless with themselves and school.

The reality is, this epidemic infects many girls in our schools, and unfortunately, adults are blind to it. This is a senseless act of violence that should not happen to anyone. School should be a place to learn, make friends and grow. Instead, for some, it is a place of on-going anxiety and suffering; a place where hallways are filled with pushing, teasing and tormenting, forcing some to chose a hiding place away from the bully and away from the embarrassment.

As adults, teachers, caregivers, community leaders and parents, we have an important job to do; we must diminish the feelings of helplessness. Children are by no means helpless, because the bully is not unstoppable. We must be here to help them, though. Our commitment must be to help, and our children must know this.

Girls will continue to be victims and bullied if parents and teachers continue to brush it off as "It's just a girl thing." This is more than that. This is ruining the lives of our children and their sense of safety and social belonging, which is something that children need in order to develop to their full potential.

Our girls need to be empowered and nurtured in their chosen strengths, but that nurturing and help begins with our own knowledge of our children and how well we look out for their well-being.

28

Resources for Parents and Teachers

As parents and teachers, we must open our eyes to the signs of relational aggression and bullying. ~Yvette Michelle Apodaca

Parents and teachers play a powerful role in identifying and intervening in bullying and relational aggression. If they choose to ignore it, though, we will continue to lose girls to this horrible epidemic. We must empower our children at a young age. We much teach them that they are worthy and instill a healthy and strong self esteem.

Unfortunately, bullies may still find a way to overpower and manipulate to the point of finding weakness in their victim. As parents and teachers, we must open our eyes to the signs of relational aggression and bullying. Given all the research gathered, I have discussed the signs that a victim may reveal in Chapter 9. Please, carefully go over this, because it can give a great over-all view of what to look for.

Just because a child may not tell an adult that they are being bullied, that doesn't mean that we can't be observant enough to catch it. Children speak in five different ways: through their body-language, their facial expressions, their eyes, tone of voice, and words. Sometimes, their words are an excuse or cover for what they are really trying to say, so don't dismiss changes in a child's behavior as merely a phase that will pass.

Even the best efforts to build a girl's sense of inner safety and confidence can be undone when she finds herself in unfamiliar physical or emotional territory, and the finest friendship skills are no assurance that relational aggression will never impact her life. There will always be other girls who feel insecure and threatened by others and respond in an aggressive way. Even the earliest, mildest episodes of relational aggression need to be dealt with, promptly and effectively.

Here are some strategies that are agreed upon by many sociologists:

- <u>Step in Early</u>: Take action to squelch problem behaviors, before they escalate into relational aggression that affects entire groups of girls.
- <u>Develop her anti-relational aggression skills</u>: Insecurity and fear are fertile ground for growing relational aggression behaviors. Identifying and celebrating a girl's strengths can make the difference between her being overcome when targeted by relational aggression and her growing stronger.
- <u>Safe Places, Safe People</u>: Teach young girls to remove themselves from situations where harassment is occurring.
- <u>Work Through the Behaviors</u>: It helps girls who are victims of relational aggression to come to understand that not all children feel emotionally secure, and those who do not often bully others. Encourage young girls to have empathy for the aggressor, who feels as insecure as the victim she targets.

I would suggest parents and teachers to do their own research about bullying and relational aggression on the internet. It is full of great articles that can be of great value, as well as a variety of point of views that can shed even more light on the subject.

I would include a list of specific websites, but unfortunately, websites are not concrete and can be taken down at any time. So, a great place to start research is a reliable search engine. Here are some key words that will bring up a variety of great pieces of information:

Bullying	Relational Aggression
Girl Bullying	Bullying Facts
Bullying Worksheets	Bullying Gone Wrong
Bullying Types	Bullying Cases
Bullying Questions	Bullying Movies
Bullying Girls	Bullying Help
Bullying Prevention Activities	Bullying Resources
Bullying Quotes	Bullying Videos
Bullying Handouts	Bullying Hotline
Bullying Online Activities	Bullying Effects
Bullying Gov	Bullying Comics
Bullying Activities for Kids	Relational Aggression in Girls
Bullying Activities for Elementary	Bullying Statistics
Bullying Books for Kids	Bullying Defined for Kids
Bullying Stories	Bullying News Articles
Relational Bullying	Bullying Curriculum
Bullying Classroom Activities	Relational Aggression Examples

I also suggest going to video sites, like Youtube, to look up similar keywords. You will find many different short films and documentaries on the subject of bullying and relational aggression. These can help you understand what victims are going through and how serious some of these incidents are.

Also, I do have a small list of books that might be helpful:

Brave New Girls by Janette Gadberg and Beth Hatlen

Odd Girl Out by Rachel Simmons

Reviving Ophelia by Mary Pipher Ballantine

Meeting at the Crossroads by Harvard University Press

The Bully, the Bullied and the Bystander by Barbara Coloroso

Queen Bees and Wannabees by Rosalind Wiseman

Girl Wars by Cheryl Dellasega and Charisse Nixon

There are many resources out there to assist us as parents and educators, and others can include joining an online Forum board, where you can interact with other parents and educators. We are all a team that has one goal in mind: to help our children.

Our world has never before been a place where worldwide embarrassment and harassment could take place. It is, now, though. Bullies take advantage of that, and it is up to us to counteract it.

No matter what, never give up on your child. Your love and concern for them will teach them a valuable lesson in life. They are not alone, they are not worthless, and they can have a bright future.

ACKNOWLEDGEMENTS

I would first like to thank God for the guidance, love, and strength that he has given me.

To my beautiful mother, Lucy Apodaca, who always told me that I can do anything I put my mind to. Who is not only my mother, but my friend and the wind beneath my wings. Without my mother, I don't know how I could have ever accomplished so much.

To my sisters, Melinda, Lisa and Sylvia, you have been through everything with me, and you made sure to support me through it all. I thank you.

To my brother, Art, who gave himself unconditionally, so that I could continue my education. What you do never goes unnoticed.

To Pacific Oaks College, a place that not only granted me a Master's degree, but a place that humbled me and taught me about life as it should be.

To Ms. Bernheimer, thank you for all of your support through the writing process of my thesis, that is now a published book!

I would like to thank Mr. Moe Anthony of "Disturbed Poetry." You believed in me and the potential of my book. Thank you for your continued support and light. You are surely a gem in my life! Thank you for introducing me to an amazing publisher and editor.

To an amazing publishing company "True Beginnings Publishing," with Selina Ahnert Lamken. Thank you for your patience through this process and for the amazing work that you did. You brought my vision to life. Your passion for this topic was heartwarming. You are a beautiful, beautiful soul.

Thank you to all my supporters and readers. I appreciate you and your interest in my book and for helping me on my journey to help fight the horrible epidemic of bullying.

About the Author

Yvette grew up in East Los Angeles, California. She now resides in West Covina, California.

She is the mother of three beautiful daughters and the grandmother of three beautiful grandchildren. Yvette has been working in the child care field for over 25 years and now operates her own business, "In Our Hands," which is a consulting business for child care centers. She has also been a college professor for eight years, teaching child development classes.

Yvette's passion is working with children and families. She now holds a B.A. in Child Development, a Master's in Human Development, and is currently working on a Master's in Marriage and Family Therapy.

Printed in Great Britain
by Amazon